The Disciple's Prayer

LEARNING TO PRAY FROM JESUS

Tommy Meador

Northwood Publishing
North Charleston, South Carolina

Copyright © 2018 by Tommy Meador

All rights reserved. No part of this publication may be reproduced, distributed or transmitted in any form or by any means, including photocopying, recording, or other electronic or mechanical methods, without the prior written permission of the publisher, except in the case of brief quotations embodied in critical reviews and certain other noncommercial uses permitted by copyright law. For permission requests, write to the publisher, addressed "Attention: Permissions Coordinator," at tdmeador@gmail.com.

Scripture quotations are from The Holy Bible, English Standard Version® (ESV®), copyright © 2001 by Crossway, a publishing ministry of Good News Publishers. Used by permission. All rights reserved.

Cover design by Amanda Evans

Book Layout ©2018 BookDesignTemplates.com

Ordering Information:
Quantity sales. Special discounts are available on quantity purchases by churches, associations, and others. For details contact tdmeador@gmail.com.

The Disciple's Prayer/ Tommy Meador. — 2nd ed.

ISBN-13: 978-0615897431
ISBN-10: 0615897436

To Staci, my beloved wife, who constantly encourages me to learn at the feet of Jesus.

To be a Christian without prayer is no more possible than to be alive without breathing.
Martin Luther

Contents

Introduction	1
Chapter 1: Why Pray?	7
Chapter 2: Who Are You Talking To?	27
Chapter 3: Hallowing God's Name	45
Chapter 4: Longing for a Kingdom	65
Chapter 5: Your Will Be Done	85
Chapter 6: Give Us Our Daily Bread	105
Chatper 7: Forgiveness	125
Chatper 8: Lord Protect Us	147
Chapter 9: Now What?	167

Introduction

ONE OF MY FAVORITE stories in church history is of Jeremiah Lanphier. Born in 1809, Lanphier converted to Christ in 1842 in a church in Lower Manhattan under the preaching of Charles Finney. Lanphier worked as a businessman for twenty years before being hired by the North Dutch Church to work as a local missionary. On July 1, 1857 he began his assignment with the church, and he hit the streets of New York to share the Gospel. He saw few conversions, but that did not stifle his passion to see people surrender to Christ.

As a former businessman, Lanphier decided to invite businessmen to a weekly lunch-hour prayer meeting at the North Dutch Church. He sent flyers all over the city in an attempt to get businessmen to attend his noon prayer meeting. On September 23, 1857, Lanphier prepared a third-floor classroom in the North Dutch Church for his first prayer meeting. At noon, no one was in the room but Lanphier. You can imagine Lanphier's discouragement. He had labored diligently to advertise the prayer meeting, but it seemed as if all his labor was in vain. It seemed as if none of the local businessmen shared Lanphier's passion for praying for the city of New York. Even though he was discouraged, Lanphier started praying alone in that classroom. A half-hour later, he heard footsteps coming up the stairs of the church. Six men entered the room and joined Lanphier in prayer. After their time of prayer and fellowship, the men committed to meet again the next week to continue praying for their city. Surprisingly, not six, but twenty men showed up the next week to pray. As the men continued to meet weekly to pray, the group continued to grow. By the first week in October, the men decided to have their prayer meetings daily, and they also had to find a new place to meet since the number of men in attendance quickly outgrew the small classroom.

The prayer group grew exponentially. Within six months, ten thousand men from all over the city met daily to pray for a move of God's Spirit in their city. Churches all over the city opened their doors for the daily prayer meetings. Before long, the prayer movement started by Lanphier expanded to other major cities across the United States, and God began to answer the prayers of His people. Lanphier began to see people in his city respond in faith to the Gospel. However, not only did people in New York begin to surrender their lives to Jesus, but within two years, one million people throughout the United States converted to faith in Christ. One man's commitment to pray for the spread of the Gospel in his city led to a nationwide revival.[1]

Doesn't that story inspire you? Every time I reflect on that story it encourages me to pray for a movement of God. However, every time I reflect on that story I am also convicted of how little passion I have for prayer. I am nothing like Jeremiah Lanphier, but I want to be. I want to be a man who desperately desires to see spiritual awakening in my church, my community, and my world. I want to be driven to my knees out of a desire to seek awakening in my heart and in the hearts of others.

I often tell my church family that every great revival in history was birthed out of prayer and proclamation of the Word of God. In our fast-paced American culture, it seems we are far too busy to do what is necessary to bring about spiritual awakening. In our churches we want programs, budgets, and buildings. We want relevant ministry for our children, concert quality music to please our ears, and engaging, entertaining sermons to hold our attention. While these things might have a place, what we often most want in a church are not the ingredients that God has used throughout church history to ignite spiritual awakening. Prayer and Gospel-centered Bible proclamation are the ingredients that ignite revival and awakening. If that's true, we need to get back to the basics in our individual lives and in the lives of our churches.

What about you? How satisfied are you with your prayer life? Are you a Jeremiah Lanphier? Are you leading people to pray passionately for the advancement of God's kingdom? You're probably like me. You probably want to pray more effectively, but you seem to pray too little or too ineffectively.

Perhaps you need some help in learning to pray more effectively so you might have a passion similar to Jeremiah Lanphier.

My goal with this book is to help you become more effective in your prayer life so you might develop a passion for spending time with the Lord. I am convinced the more passionate you become about prayer, the more you are going to fall on your knees before the Lord and challenge your brothers and sisters in Christ to do the same. What would happen in your life if you spent more time praying? What would happen in your life if you learned how to run to God in every area of your life in full dependence on Him? What would happen if you turned to the Lord in prayer when making a decision rather than turning to the wisdom of the world?

Prayer will change you, but the reality is many of us simply do not know how to pray. In the passage of Scripture known as *The Lord's Prayer*, Jesus teaches us exactly how to pray. You are undoubtedly familiar with the Lord's Prayer in Matthew 6:9-13:

> Our Father in heaven, hallowed be your name. Your kingdom come, your will be done, on earth as it is in heaven. Give us this day our daily bread, and forgive us our debts, as we also have forgiven our debtors. And lead us not into temptation, but deliver us from evil.

We often think of the Lord's Prayer as a ritualistic prayer to be prayed at weddings and funerals, but this prayer is much more than a ritualistic prayer. In this prayer (which should more accurately be called the Disciple's Prayer), Jesus literally teaches us how to pray effectively. We need to sit at the feet of Jesus and let Him teach us!

I'm inviting you to join me on a journey to mine the riches of the Disciple's Prayer to discover how we can become more effective in our prayer lives. Can you think of a better investment of your time than learning how to communicate with the God of all creation who has called you into a relationship with Him through faith in Christ?

In the following pages, we will walk through the Disciple's Prayer phrase by phrase exposing each petition's meaning and discussing practical ways you can apply each petition of the Disciple's Prayer to your own prayer life. The best way to read this book is with a friend or a small group. In each chapter I have included a series of questions for you to discuss in a small group setting. Use these questions as a starting point for discussion. You'll likely find as you work through this book with a friend or a small group, you will have plenty to discuss. Let the questions in each chapter guide your conversation. You can obviously read this book apart from a small group, but I am convinced that our most significant spiritual growth takes place in a community of believers. You will greatly benefit from dialoging with others about what you learn in this book. You're likely to learn more by discussing this book with others than you are by simply reading this book by yourself.

As you study the Disciple's Prayer and apply its truths to your life, I pray your desire to spend time communicating with the Lord will grow exponentially. I pray individuals, small groups, and churches will once again discover that prayer is our lifeline as followers of Jesus Christ. I pray we will experience a prayer revival among our churches as we cry out to God in absolute surrender and dependency. I pray for a longing in our lives to spend more time in God's presence than we spend longing to be entertained by church programs. Will you sit at the feet of Jesus with me and allow Him to teach us how to pray to our Father?

[1]

Why Pray?

I RECENTLY READ THAT prayer is the most natural thing a believer can do. If it's the most natural thing a believer can do, why is it so unnatural for me? I'm inspired by some of my heroes in the faith like John Wesley and E.M. Bounds who would rise early in the morning and pray for several hours before they started their day. Can you imagine waking up at four in the morning and praying until seven? That was pretty common for Bounds, who was a confederacy chaplain during the Civil War and an author of many books on prayer. For me, it's a struggle to get up by six, and while I have disciplined myself to begin every day praying and studying Scripture, I am far from being like Wesley or Bounds. I hate to admit that many mornings I rush through my time of Scripture reading and prayer so I can get on with my day. I have definitely made progress in my prayer life, but I have a long way to go. I often find myself distracted when I pray.

My mind wanders. I have a hard time staying focused. Sometimes I feel like I'm just repeating the same prayers over and over again each day. I need to learn how to have a deeper and more intimate prayer life. The reality is that neither I, nor you, can read Scripture without becoming convinced that prayer is vitally important in the life of the believer. If prayer is so important, we need to learn how to pray effectively.

Take an evaluation of your own life. How important is prayer to you? Perhaps you have been in church for a number of years, and you have heard sermon after sermon about how important prayer is, but it is so difficult for you to spend time with God. Maybe you do not know how to pray, or maybe developing discipline is not easy for you. You know God desires to commune with you, and you have heard story after story about how God miraculously answered someone's prayers. You want that to be your story, but it's not. You have heard of people rising early in the morning to spend uninterrupted time with the Lord, but your life is busy. You hit the ground running every morning, and by time you lay your head on the pillow at night you are out like a light. I know you are busy, but you cannot afford not to spend time in God's presence on a regular basis. Prayer is your lifeline! Let me share with you why prayer is so important.

1. *Are you satisfied with your prayer life? Why or why not? What are some challenges to your prayer life?*

Prayer is Powerful

Prayer is so important because prayer is powerful. You do not have to look too far in Scripture to come to the conclusion that prayer is powerful. Page after page you find examples of God answering the prayers of His children so He might display His glory, and so people might stand in awe of His greatness. Take Joshua for example. In Joshua 10, Joshua and the Israelites were in the heat of battle. The sun began to go down, but the battle was not over. Joshua needed more time, so he raised his voice to the Lord and said, "Sun, stand still at Gibeon, and moon, in the Valley of Aijalon" (Joshua 10:12). Do you know what happened? The sun stopped setting and the moon stopped rising! Joshua 10:13 says, "And the sun stood still, and the moon stopped, until the nation took vengeance on their enemies." Based on this passage of Scripture wouldn't you say that prayer is powerful? Joshua made a bold request, and God answered.

We say we believe God answers prayers, and plenty of Bible passages teach us that God desires to answer the prayers of His children. Jesus said in John 15:7, "If you abide in me, and my words abide in you, ask whatever you wish, and it will be done for you." What an amazing promise! The Apostle John wrote,

> And this is the confidence that we have toward him, that if we ask anything according to his will he hears us. And if we know that he hears us in whatever we ask, we know we have the requests that we have asked of him. (1 John 5:14-15)

Do you pray like you believe God is able to do what is seemingly impossible? Right now you might be facing a situation that seems impossible. You might have a loved one who is fighting cancer, or maybe you are in a marriage that seems like it is beyond God's help. Are you crying out to God and asking Him to do the impossible? Do you believe He is able to do the seemingly impossible? As we study the Disciple's Prayer, we will discover that God doesn't always answer our prayers according to our will, but certainly He is able to do anything we might ask. He always powerfully answers prayers according to His will.

King Jehoshaphat saw God answer his prayers in a powerful way. In 2 Chronicles 20 Jehoshaphat learned that several nations had joined to attack his people. He knew it was humanly impossible for his army to defeat the combined armies of the enemy nations. Jehoshaphat's first course of action was not to devise an evacuation plan to get the people out of Judah. Rather, his first course of action was prayer. In 2 Chronicles 20:12 Jehoshaphat said to the Lord, "For we are powerless against this great horde that is coming against us. We do not know what to do, but our eyes are on you." God heard the prayer of Jehoshaphat, and He answered in a miraculous way. God told Jehoshaphat that He would fight his battle for him. This promise fueled Jehoshaphat's confidence. Jehoshaphat was so confident that the Lord would deliver his nation that on the day of battle he sent the choir out on the front lines. Can you imagine? As the enemy army approached expecting to hear the sound of warriors waiting for battle they heard a choir singing praise songs instead! I imagine as the enemy army approached Judah and saw this choir that had come out for battle, they felt confident this was going to be an even easier victory than they had imagined. However, it was not an easy victory for the enemy nations. Instead it was an easy victory for Judah! Verse 22 says,

> And when they began to sing and praise, the Lord set an ambush against the men of Ammon, Moab, and Mount Seir, who had come against Judah so that they were routed.

What a story! You cannot come away from this story not believing prayer is powerful. Do you and I pray like we believe God is our only hope? Undoubtedly you have been in some situations that seemed hopeless. Where do you turn when you are without hope? Relatives? Friends? Counselors? Self-help books? Or, do you turn to the only One who is able to give you hope in hopeless situations?

Let me give you one more Old Testament example of God's power at work through prayer. In the Book of Ezra, the Israelites began to return to Jerusalem to rebuild their homeland after being in exile for seventy years. As the Israelites returned, the Persian king sent his own soldiers with the Israelites as they made their way back to Jerusalem to protect them from enemy nations that did not want to see them return. When the time came for Ezra to go back to Jerusalem, he did not want the protection. He believed that God was perfectly able to protect him. Ezra did not need the king's soldiers when the God of all creation was on his side. Ezra prayed for protection.

> Then I proclaimed a fast there, at the river Ahava, that we might humble ourselves before our God, to seek from him a safe journey for ourselves, our children, and all our goods. For I was ashamed to ask the king for a band of soldiers and horsemen to protect us against the enemy on our way, since we had told the king, "The hand of our God is for good on all who seek him, and the power of his wrath is against all who forsake him." So we fasted and implored our God for this, and he listened to our entreaty. (Ezra 8:21-23)

Do you and I pray as if we believe God is our only protector? We desperately need protection. We need protection from the evil one. We need protection from those who try to steal our joy. We need protection from ourselves. Where do you run for protection? Who or what is your shield? Is it the only One who is able to protect?

Do you see a pattern emerging in these stories? Men and women in Scripture believed in a powerful God, and they, trusting that God would answer their prayers, cried out to Him in faith. God answered and people were amazed.

I have given you three examples of men whose bold prayers were answered miraculously by God, but the examples in Scripture are countless. If you surveyed Scripture to discover how God answered the prayers of His people, you would be absolutely amazed. Over and over again in Scripture God worked powerfully on behalf of His people. James, the half-brother of Jesus, encouraged early Christians to pray because he was convinced of the power of prayer. He wrote, "The prayer of a righteous person has great power as it is working" (James 5:17). If you are a follower of Jesus Christ, you are a righteous person. You are not righteous because of anything you have done. You are righteous because of what Christ has done for you. Jesus is fully human and fully God, and He did what you are not able to do. He lived perfectly. Not once did He rebel against His Father. He perfectly kept His Father's commands, and He went to the cross and died in your place as a perfect sacrifice for your sins. Three days later He rose from the dead proving that He is indeed fully human and fully God. His death and resurrection also paved the way for all who believe to live eternally.

All who confess their sins and surrender their lives completely to His will are forgiven of their sins and brought into an intimate relationship with the God of all creation. All who trust in Christ through faith are clothed in His righteousness. If you are a believer, you are righteous because of Jesus and not because of anything you have done. The righteousness of Christ covers your unrighteousness, and your prayers have great power. If that's true, why not pray more? Why not approach God with confidence and boldness?

2. Have you trusted in Christ alone for your salvation? Are you depending on His righteousness to save you or are you depending on your righteousness?

3. Does your prayer life, and does the prayer life of your church, demonstrate a belief in a God who is powerful? Why or why not?

4. *Why do you think Christians fail to cry out to God in prayer especially when Scripture is clear that God is powerful and desires to work in the lives of His children?*

Prayer is Necessary

Another reason prayer is so important is because prayer is necessary. Prayer is necessary to grow in intimacy with the Lord, and prayer is necessary to know God's will for your life. When I read the Gospels I am always amazed at the number of times Jesus prayed. Before Jesus began His public ministry He spent forty days in the wilderness fasting and praying. Matthew 4:1-2 says, "Then Jesus was led up by the Spirit into the wilderness to be tempted by the devil. And after fasting forty days and forty nights, he was hungry." Mark reports in the very first chapter of his Gospel that Jesus prayed early in the morning. Mark 1:35 says, "And rising very early in the morning, while it was still dark, he departed and went out to a desolate place, and there he prayed." Luke 5:16 says, "But he would withdraw to desolate places and pray." After Jesus fed the five thousand, Jesus got away to pray. Mark 6:45-46 says, "Immediately he made his disciples get into the boat and go before him to the other side, to Bethsaida, while he dismissed the crowd. And after he had taken leave of them, he went up on the mountain to pray." In Luke 6, right before Jesus chose the twelve apostles, He prayed all night. Luke 6:12

says, "In these days he went out to the mountain to pray, and all night he continued in prayer to God." In John 17, Jesus prayed what is known as the *high priestly prayer*. In this prayer Jesus specifically prayed for His followers. In Mark 14, on the eve of His crucifixion, Jesus intensely prayed in the Garden of Gethsemane. On the cross, Jesus cried out to the Father. In Luke 23:34, Jesus cried to the Father from the cross, "Father, forgive them, for they know not what they do." As Jesus absorbed the wrath of God for the sins of humanity He cried, "My God, my God, why have you forsaken me?" (Mark 15:34)

5. *Have you ever considered how often Jesus prayed in the Gospels? Can you think of other examples of Jesus praying in the Gospels? Why do you think Jesus prayed so often?*

Isn't this amazing? The One who was fully human and fully divine, the God-man, prayed and prayed often. He began His mornings by rising before daylight to spend time with the Father. He got away from the crowds to be with the Father. At times He prayed all night, and when His most difficult moments came, He ran to the Father's presence. Why would the One who is all-powerful and all-knowing need to pray?

Jesus had an intimate relationship with the Father, and while He was on earth, prayer was the evidence of His intimacy with the Father. Orthodox Christians believe that God is triune. God as Trinity is an extremely difficult doctrine to explain because of its mysterious nature, but in essence Christians worship one God. While we worship only one God, our God exists in three distinct persons: Father, Son, and Holy Spirit. Perfect intimacy exists among the Trinity. When God the Son, Jesus, was on this earth, He maintained perfect unity with the Father, and His prayer life demonstrated that He desired intimacy with God the Father. The only time Jesus' intimacy with the Father was broken was when Jesus went to the cross and suffered the wrath of God. When Jesus cried out, "My God, my God, why have you forsaken me?" He was experiencing separation from the Father for the only time in all of eternity. Throughout His life, prayer was necessary for Jesus because it was the evidence of His intimate relationship with the Father.

Prayer is necessary for you because through prayer you cultivate intimacy with the Father. We will discuss this further in the next chapter but understand that because of your faith in Christ you are now a child of God. You have been adopted into His family, and your Father desires a relationship with you. John writes, "See what kind of love the Father has given to us, that we should be called children of God; and so we are" (1 John 3:1).

How can you cultivate a relationship with your Father if you do not spend time with Him? The more you spend time with the Lord in prayer, the more you will grow in intimacy with your heavenly Father.

6. *How would you describe your relationship with the Father? Would you say that you are growing not just in a knowledge of Him, but in intimacy with Him? Outside of direct communication with God through hearing Him from His Word and responding to Him in prayer, can you think of other ways to grow in intimacy with God?*

Prayer was necessary for Jesus not only because of His desire to continue to cultivate intimacy with the Father, but also because He was submitted to the will of the Father. (We will dive into God's will in detail in a later chapter.) Jesus was fully God, and the Bible is clear that while He was on earth He did not consider equality with God the Father a thing to be grasped. The Apostle Paul gives us a glimpse into the character of Christ in Philippians 2:5-7. Paul writes,

> Have this mind among yourselves, which is yours in Christ Jesus, who, though he was in the form of God, did not count equality with God a thing to be grasped, but emptied himself, by taking the form of a servant, being born in the likeness of men. And being found in human form, he humbled himself by becoming obedient to the point of death, even death on a cross.

Doesn't the humility of Jesus amaze you? Think about it. If you were all-powerful and all-knowing, how would you live on this earth? Would you live as a peasant? Would you live as a servant? Would you live for the will of another? That is exactly what Jesus did. The One who has been with the Father for all of eternity, and the One for whom all things are created willingly chose to live as a homeless vagabond. He willingly chose to serve the people who had sinned against Him by laying down His life for them. He willingly chose to do His Father's will. The One who has been given the name that is above all names and is highly exalted (Philippians 2:8) was not on this earth to do His will but rather to do His Father's will. Jesus needed to spend time in the Father's presence to stay in alignment with the Father's will. As He prayed, He was following the Father's lead by listening to the Father's directions and obeying. For Jesus, prayer was an act of submission to the Father.

You are not on this earth to accomplish your will. I'm sure you have heard preachers tell you that before, and I'm sure you have read that for yourself in Scripture. Nevertheless, we have a hard time living for God's will rather than our own will. Life is not about accomplishing your goals or chasing your dreams. Life is not about making a name for yourself or collecting as many material possessions as possible. Have you ever noticed how many times we pray in an attempt to coerce God to submit to our will as if we are the one who are supposed to call the shots? We will pray things like, "God I really need this job. I really need You to come through for me" rather than praying, "God, where can I best serve You? What job will give me the best opportunity to make much of Jesus?"

Never forget you were created and redeemed to accomplish the will of God. You have been placed on this earth to accomplish the purpose God has for you. How do you know why God has placed you on earth? How do you know His will for your life? You pray and ask God to show you from His Word how He desires you to submit to His will. You search the Scriptures, and you ask God to reveal His will to you. As you pray and put yourself under God's Word, God's Spirit communicates with your heart and helps you to discern the will of the Father. Romans 8:26-28 says,

> Likewise the Spirit helps us in our weakness. For we do not know what to pray for as we ought, but the Spirit himself intercedes for us with groanings too deep for words. And he who searches hearts knows what is the mind of the Spirit, because the Spirit intercedes for the saints according to the will of God.

7. Evaluate your prayer life. Does your prayer life demonstrate that you are submitted to the will of God, or does your prayer life demonstrate that you are trying to get God to submit to your will?

When I read through the Gospels, I discover I'm not the only one amazed at how Jesus prayed. The way Jesus prayed also amazed His disciples. They had never seen someone pray so earnestly, someone so disciplined to get up every morning before sunrise to pray, or someone willing to stay up all night in prayer. When Jesus prayed in the Garden of

Gethsemane on the eve of His crucifixion, He asked the disciples to stay up and pray with Him, but they could not stay awake. Jesus' prayer life was much more advanced than their prayer lives. As they witnessed Jesus praying, they wanted to know more. They wanted to know how to pray like Him. They wanted to know how to pray earnestly and with power. Luke 11:1 says,

> Now Jesus was praying in a certain place and when he finished, one of his disciples said to him, "Lord teach us to pray, as John taught his disciples."

This seems like a logical request. The disciples yearned for the same intimacy with the Father that Jesus had, and who better to teach them to draw near to the Father than the One who had perfect fellowship with the Father? It would make sense for us, as well, to run to Jesus and ask Him to teach us to pray if we yearn for intimacy with our Lord.

8. In your desire to be more effective in your prayer life, have you ever stopped and asked Jesus, "Will you teach me to pray?" Why or why not?

Prayer is Transformative

Prayer is so important because prayer is transformative. When the disciples asked Jesus to teach them to pray, Jesus responded by giving them what we call the Lord's Prayer. You can find the Lord's Prayer in Luke 11:1-4 and Matthew 6:9-13. While we most often call this prayer the Lord's Prayer, it is probably better described as the Disciple's Prayer. This is a prayer intended as a model for followers of Jesus as we learn how to pray like Jesus. If you have been a Christian for a while, you probably already know this prayer. If you grew up in church, you might have been a part of a more formal congregation which recited this prayer every Sunday, or maybe you have recited the Disciple's Prayer at a wedding. While reciting the Disciple's Prayer is not wrong, this prayer was not given for us to recite primarily as a ritual. Jesus gave us the Disciple's Prayer to teach us how to approach the God of all creation. Learning to use the Disciple's Prayer as a model in your own prayer life will transform the way you pray.

If you allow the Disciple's Prayer to be a model for your own prayer life, then the focus of your prayers will be on God, not you. The Disciple's Prayer is perfectly balanced. The prayer contains six petitions. The first three are completely focused on God. The Disciple's Prayer challenges us to praise God's name, pray for the advancement of His kingdom, and pray for His perfect will to be done. Petitions four, five, and six focus on our needs. If you begin your prayers focused on God's greatness, His mission, and His will, don't you think it will drastically affect the way you pray for your needs? If your focus is on God, instead of you, when you pray, don't you think you will be more likely to pray according to His will rather than praying according to your will?

If you look at Matthew's account of the Disciple's Prayer, Jesus gave His followers this model prayer as He preached what we call the *Sermon on the Mount*. Right before this prayer Jesus warned His followers about what prayer should not be like. He told them not to pray like hypocrites and pagans. Pagans babble with vain repetitions thinking their gods are impressed by their many words. The Pharisees, who Jesus called hypocrites, stood on the street corners and prayed so everyone could see how spiritual they were. Jesus is not impressed with many words, and He is not impressed with a desire to be seen by others. Rather, what pleases Jesus is a heart that genuinely desires to exalt God and follow His will. This is why Jesus tells His followers to go into their closets, shut their doors, and pray to God in secret. Prayer is not a ritual, and prayer is not a religious show. Prayer is a time to seek the Father's perfect will. The Disciple's Prayer is so transformative because in this prayer Jesus teaches us how to exalt God and seek His will above everything else.

I know prayer can be a struggle, but it is so important in the life of a believer. If you and I will learn to discipline ourselves to spend time in God's presence, we will experience intimacy with Him like never before. We will also experience the power of God in a way that we have never experienced. What would happen if not only you got serious about seeking

God through prayer, but your entire church got serious about seeking God through prayer?

The Moravians were a group of about three hundred believers who knew the importance of prayer. These believers fled from Saxony in 1722 because of persecution and made their home in Moravia on a piece of property owned by Nikolas von Zizendorf, who became their leader. The Moravians were passionate about making Christ known to the nations, and they believed they had to remain completely unified to do so. Living on the same piece of property, sharing their possessions like the early church in Acts 2, and enjoying daily fellowship seemed like a sure way to build the unity they thought was so important for the spread of the Gospel. Obviously, unity is essential for believers, but unity did not come as easily as the Moravians thought it would. Within a few weeks of living together on Ziznedorf's estate these believers began feuding with each other. The fighting broke Zizendorf's heart, and he called the Moravian believers to prayer. Zizendorf's call to prayer resulted in an ongoing twenty-four hour prayer vigil. Every hour, two men and two women prayed, twenty-four hours a day. The prayer vigil did not cease, and revival broke out among the people. People repented of sin and reconciled previously broken relationships. The Moravians did not stop praying. Every day for one hundred years the prayer vigil went uninterrupted![1]

Undoubtedly, the Moravians one-hundred-year prayer vigil fueled their zeal for missions. By 1760, as a result of praying together and living out the Gospel together, this group of three hundred believers who had moved to Moravia grew to over six hundred believers. Even more impressive than their growth was the fact that by 1760 the Moravians had sent out 226 missionaries to places such as Greenland, Lapland, Georgia, Surinam, the Guinea Coast of Africa, South Africa, Amsterdam, Algeria, the native North Americans, Ceylon, Romania, and Constantinople.[2] In a time in which international missions was unheard of, this was a remarkable feat by a people who through constant prayer experienced being empowered by the Holy Spirit to accomplish much for the glory of God. What would happen if we devoted ourselves to prayer like the Moravians did?

Prayer is powerful, prayer is necessary, and prayer is transformative. When we pray we will experience intimacy with God, and our hearts will be brought into alignment with His will. When our hearts are in alignment with His will, we will be empowered by His Spirit to do things even greater than we can imagine. Paul writes in Ephesians 3:20-21,

> Now to him who is able to do far more abundantly than all that we ask or think, according to the power at work within us, to him be glory in the church and in Christ Jesus throughout all generations, forever and ever. Amen.

If God is able to do more than we can ask or think, then let us begin seeking Him through prayer. Let us ask Him to do more than we can ask or think so that His glory will be made known in this world.

As we dive into the Disciple's Prayer, my prayer is that you will be challenged in your own prayer life, and that you will have a renewed desire to spend time in intimate conversation with the God who loves you. I challenge you, as we begin this study, to read the Disciple's Prayer each day with a prayerful heart. As you read it each day, simply ask Jesus to teach you to pray in such a way that you might experience deeper intimacy with Him, and that you also might experience His power at work in you and through you.

9. *Would you say your prayer life is transformative? Why or why not? Read Matthew 6:5-13. Do you see evidence in your life of praying like a hypocrite or a pagan? Why do you think it is so important to pray in secret?*

10. *Spend time asking Jesus to teach you to pray so you might experience intimacy with Him, and so you might experience His power at work in you and through you.*

[2]

Who Are You Talking To?

An Unexpected Address

THE DISCIPLE'S PRAYER BEGINS in a way that is completely familiar to us, but if you were a first century Jew, the way Jesus begins this prayer would have caused you to cringe. Perhaps a first century Jew would have been more comfortable if Jesus would have said, "When you pray, pray 'Our Creator in heaven.'" Addressing God as Creator would be completely accurate. He is our Creator, and He should be worshipped as Creator. The psalmist writes,

> Praise him, sun and moon, praise him, all you shining stars! Praise him, you highest heavens, and you waters above the heavens! Let them praise the name of the Lord! For he commanded and they were created. (Psalm 148:3-5)

Think about it. If God was just your Creator, what kind of relationship would you have with Him? Think of things you have created. If you are a cook, maybe you have created a delicious meal. Or, if you are a woodworker, maybe you have created a beautiful back porch swing. Maybe you are an artist, and you have painted a lovely landscape. Undoubtedly, you have found some satisfaction in what you have created, but what happened after you stood back and admired what you created? You moved on with your life. After creating a delicious dinner, ten hours later you were back in the kitchen making breakfast. After putting the finishing touches on that back-porch swing, you stepped back, admired what you made, and then moved on to your next building project. After you painted that serene landscape, you began working on something more abstract. The point is, after you created whatever it was you created, you stepped back, admired your work for a moment, and moved on. Your relationship with your creation only lasted until your creation was completed.

If God is just Creator, what obligation does He have to those He has created once He has finished creating? What kind of relationship is He obligated to have with His creation if He is just Creator? If God is just Creator, why would He not simply move on to the next project?

Maybe a first century Jew would have been more comfortable if Jesus began this prayer by saying, "When you pray, pray 'Our King in heaven.'" That would be an accurate way to address God. He is our King. He is the only King. God reigns and rules over this universe according to His will, and no one can thwart His will. Psalm 47:1-2 says, "Clap your hands, all peoples! Shout to God with loud songs of joy! For the Lord, the Most High, is to be feared, a great king over all the earth."

What kind of relationship do you have with a king? We do not have a king in America, but we have a president. Have you tried to get in touch with the President lately? You cannot do it! When I was in the third grade I wrote a letter to the President. I had just finished reading in *Weekly Reader* (Do they still have those?) about the dangers of pollution. I was an outraged third grader, so I wrote a letter to President George H.W. Bush asking him to do something to save our environment. I put the letter in the mail, and proudly patted myself on the back for doing something to help America. I waited and waited for a reply from President Bush. Finally, after weeks of waiting, I came home from school one afternoon to find a large envelope from the Whitehouse on the kitchen counter. I ripped open the envelope only to find a glossy portrait of President Bush. I did not want a portrait of the President. I wanted a response to my letter. That day I learned that I do not have access to the President of the United States.

Certainly God is King, but could we approach Him if He's just King? What right do we have to approach the King of the Universe? What right do we have to come into His presence and interrupt Him to ask anything of Him? After all, if He's just King, isn't He much too busy running the universe to be bothered by us? What right do we have to petition the one who rules and reigns according to His will?

Do not misunderstand me. One of the major problems within the church today is a failure to recognize God as King.

We too often think we are the kings of our own lives, and we do not want anyone reigning and ruling over us. Make no mistake about it: you are not in charge. God is the King who sits on His throne and who rules over your life. Your knee will bow to Him in submission, either in this life or the next. Our God is not a King who is unapproachable. He is completely approachable because He is more than our King. He is our Father.

Think about what Jesus says. He calls us to address God as Father. For those of us who have been in church for most of our lives, and even for those of us whose exposure to church is limited, we are used to hearing God described as Father. We gloss over the phrase, "Our Father, in heaven," without any thought of the profound implications of what we are saying when we utter, "Our Father." If you lived as a first century Jew rather than a twenty-first century believer, you would have been absolutely appalled at how Jesus addressed God. Jews did not think of God as their personal Father. They thought of God as distant and unapproachable, but Jesus teaches His disciples, and us, to address God just like we would address our earthly fathers: with a sure knowledge that our Father desires an intimate relationship with us in which He freely gives us what is best for us.

To be sure, the writers of the Old Testament believed God was their Father, but not in the sense in which Jesus calls us to pray to God in the Disciple's Prayer. In the thirty-nine books of the Old Testament God is referred to as *Father* fourteen times, and when God is called Father in the Old Testament it is in reference to God being Father of the nation of

Israel.[1] In other words, God was the Father of the Israelite nation, but He was not thought of as an intimate, personal father of individual Jewish people. In a sense, it would be like us calling George Washington the father of the United States. In some ways we attribute to George Washington the establishment of our democracy, but none of us have a personal relationship with George Washington. After all, he's dead. It's not even possible. However, God is alive, and He is not merely the founder of a nation. He is the lover of our souls. Jewish individuals had no concept of the kind of intimacy God desired to share with them.

Jesus shifts the paradigm. A first century Jew would never have thought to refer to God as his father in the way that Jesus does. Maybe you have heard a pastor say that the word Jesus uses most often in the Gospels to address God is the Greek word *abba*. The word *abba* was an extremely common word in Greek culture. It was the word a little child used to address his or her father. If you were a fly on the wall in a Jewish home, you would see a little girl crawling up in her daddy's lap and saying, "Abba, I love you." You would see a little boy wrestling with his daddy in the floor saying, "Abba, when I grow up, I want to be strong just like you." *Abba* was a word of intimacy and fellowship. When a child said *abba* an image of that child's father came to mind, and it was an image of safety, protection, provision, and love. If you look at the four Gospels, *Father* was the normal way Jesus referred to God. Over sixty times Jesus calls God *Father*. The only instance in which Jesus does not address God as *Father* is on the cross when Jesus cried out, "My God, my God, why have you forsaken me?"[2]

When Jesus teaches us to pray, He teaches us to address God just as we might address our earthly fathers; with the knowledge that our heavenly Father is our perfect Father who loves us infinitely more than our earthly fathers, and with the knowledge that our heavenly Father is our ultimate protector and provider. This foundational truth that God is your Father is central to your Christian faith. Reflect on the words of J.I. Packer, a former pastor and seminary professor whose writings have helped many Christians come to a greater understanding of God over the years.

> If you want to judge how well a person understands Christianity, find out how much he makes of the thought of being God's child, and having God as his Father. If this is not the thought that prompts and controls his worship and prayers and his whole outlook on life, it means that he does not understand Christianity very well at all. For everything that Christ taught, everything that makes the New Testament new, and better than the Old, everything that is distinctively Christian as opposed to merely Jewish, is summed up in the knowledge of the Fatherhood of God. "Father" is the Christian name for God.[3]

1. When you think of God are you more likely to think of Him as Creator, King, or Father? Why?

2. How does knowing that God is your Father who desires an intimate relationship with you change the way you pray?

THE GIFT OF ADOPTION

What gives you the right to call God your Father? After all, He is Creator. What right do you have to talk to the one who created you? Aren't you simply a pawn in His hands for Him to use as He desires? Do you have any right to say anything to Him? Besides that, God is King. Who has the right to come into the presence of a King and ask anything? How is it that the one who is Creator and King is also your Father? God is your Father because He adopted you.

We do not talk enough about adoption in the church, but adoption is exactly what took place in your life the moment you trusted Christ as Lord and Savior of your life. You were adopted into God's family, and you were given all the rights and privileges that come along with being a child of a father.

As a pastor, over the years I've had the opportunity to witness lots of families in my congregations adopt children. I love talking to couples who are going through the process of adoption. They have great anticipation and expectation in their hearts. The children they will eventually bring into their homes will be their own children. These mothers might not have carried these infants in their wombs, and these infants might not share the same blood and chromosomes as their adoptive parents, but this does not change the reality that they will be fully children of their adoptive parents. These children will be loved by their adoptive parents just like any natural children these adoptive parents might already have or have in the future. It will be as if these children are flesh and blood with their adoptive mom and dad.

These children who have been given up by their birth parents have been rescued by parents who are willing to bring them into their home and love them as their own children. None of these children pursued their adoptive parents. Rather, their adoptive parents pursued them. Before some adopted children are ever born they are being pursued by a mom and dad who want nothing more than to bring a child into their home to love, nurture, and raise. Adoption is a work that is totally initiated by the adoptive parents. In many cases, the adoptive parent even pays for the birth mother's living expenses until the child is born on top of many other financial costs that are involved in adoption. Adoptive parents desperately want to rescue children out of less than ideal circumstances and give these children the best home possible.

This is a beautiful picture of the Gospel, because in the same way, you have been adopted by our heavenly Father through faith in Jesus Christ. You were in less than ideal circumstances. You were an orphan who could not survive in a world of sin and despair, but there was a Father who loved you, who before the foundation of the world determined that He would bring you into His family. Reflect on what Paul writes in Ephesians 1:3-6:

> Blessed be the God and Father of our Lord Jesus Christ, who has blessed us in Christ with every spiritual blessing

in the heavenly places, even as he chose us in him before the foundation of the world that we should be holy and blameless before him. In love he predestined us for adoption as sons through Jesus Christ, according to the purpose of his will, to the praise of his glorious grace, with which he has blessed us in the Beloved.

Before you ever took your first breath, the God who is Creator and King chose to adopt you and bring you into His family as His child. You did not pursue the Father. The Bible teaches in Ephesians 2:1-2 that you were dead in your trespasses and sins. I don't think we realize how bad our condition was before we came to know Christ. Paul paints a very bleak picture of our spiritual reality apart from Christ. Because you were dead to Christ you did not choose to follow Him. Instead, you chose to follow everything that was opposed to God. You chose to follow the ways of this world. You chose to follow your own passions and desires, and you chose to follow the influence of Satan himself. Before you came to know Christ, you constantly chose rebellion rather than submission to Christ.

Because of your spiritual blindness you were not able to pursue a relationship with Him, but in His grace, God sent His only begotten Son to this earth to rescue you from sin and bring you into His family. Paul writes,

> But God, being rich in mercy, because of the great love with which he loved us, even when we were dead in our trespasses, made us alive together with Christ — by grace you have been saved — and raised us up with him and seated us with him in the heavenly places in Christ Jesus... (Ephesians 2:4-6)

God chose to love you in spite of your rebellion, and He came after you by sending Jesus who brought you into a relationship the Father by giving His life as a sacrifice for your sins. Do you get it? You were pursued by a loving Father whose desire was for you to be in His family so that He might express His love to you for all of eternity.

Adoption is a blessing and a gift from God. The truth is that God could have forgiven you of your sins without adopting you into His family because not only is God the Creator and the King, He is also the Judge. He is the Great Judge of the entire universe. The Great Judge had every right to condemn you to hell because of your sin and rebellion against Him, but when you surrendered your life to Christ, the Great Judge made a legal declaration on your behalf. He declared you innocent, not because you are, but because Jesus, who was innocent, paid the penalty for your sin. We call this legal declaration *justification*. Simply put, Jesus served your time for you so you could be set free.

Justification gives us a right legal standing before God, but adoption gives us an intimate relationship with God. God could have pardoned us from all of our sins and allowed us to enjoy eternal life without actually bringing us into His family. If we were not adopted into His family, our relationship with God would be much different. We would be merely His slave. We would owe Him our allegiance and our service because He pardoned our sins. However, the Great Judge not only freed us from the penalty of our sin, He also brought us into His family because He loves us and desires an intimate relationship with us. While we do owe Him our allegiance and our service as a slave owes his master his allegiance and service, we are not merely God's slaves. We are His sons and daughters. What an awesome blessing! This blessing should cause you to worship the one who rescued you and adopted you! Consider what Paul writes in Galatians 4:4-7:

> But when the fullness of time had come, God sent forth his Son, born of woman, born under the law, to redeem those who were under the law, so that we might receive adoption as sons. And because you are sons, God has sent the Spirit of his Son into our hearts crying, "Abba! Father!" So you are no longer a slave, but a son, and if a son, then an heir through God.

You are an heir of God's kingdom through faith in Christ! Isn't that astounding? You will enjoy the same riches that Jesus Christ presently enjoys. Someday, when Christ returns, you will enjoy a glorified body, just like Christ enjoys. You will also enjoy perfect fellowship with the Father that is not hindered by sin, just as Christ enjoys. Never minimize the fact that you have been adopted by the Creator, King, and Judge of the universe.

If you have trusted Christ, the reality that God has adopted you into His family is extremely good news. Unfortunately, we live in a time in which many do not understand the love of a father. Perhaps you don't have pleasant memories of a loving father who nurtured you and raised you to be a mature follower of Christ. Maybe you were abandoned by your earthly father, and you never knew what it was like to have a father. Maybe your relationship with your father has always been on the rocks. Perhaps your father was abusive or extremely unkind in the way he talked to you. For some of you, the very mention of the word *father* brings to mind a host of hurtful memories. Be assured that while your earthly father might have failed you in a multitude of ways, your heavenly Father will never fail you. God will always be faithful to you. He will never abuse you nor will He leave you. He will never be unkind to you, and He will always nurture you and help you become what He desires you to be. God will be the Father you never had.

3. *How should the fact that you are an adopted child of God change the way you pray?*

4. *What is your reaction to the reality that God chose you for His family before you were even created you, and then pursued you through His Son?*

5. *What are some privileges of being a part of God's family?*

6. *Knowing that God is not just your judge, but also your Father, how does it affect the way you view your sin? How should you desire to live before your Father? Why?*

The Gift of the Father's Listening Ear

Knowing God is our Father has massive implications for how we pray. You can ask God anything, and you can know if what you ask God is in His best interest for your life, He will give you what you ask. Jesus' words in Matthew 7:7-11 show us just how much our Father wants to provide for us.

> Ask, and it will be given to you; seek, and you will find; knock, and it will be opened to you. For everyone who asks receives, and the one who seeks finds, and to the one who knocks it will be opened. Or which one of you, if his son asks him for bread, will give him a stone? Or if he asks for a fish, will give him a serpent? If you then, who are evil, know how to give good gifts to your children, how much more will your Father who is in heaven give good things to those who ask him!

Now, you need to understand these verses in their proper context. Jesus is not teaching us that if you ask God for anything, God is obligated to give you everything you ask. This is not an invitation to ask God for a brand-new Lamborghini or for a mansion on an isolated Caribbean island. These verses are toward the end of the Sermon on the Mount, and Jesus has been teaching His followers about the kind of obedience God desires. Their initial reaction to the radical obedience Jesus was calling them to was probably, "We can never do this! What God requires is too much for us!" That's exactly the point Jesus was making. What God requires from us is too much. We simply cannot do all that God requires of us because of our proclivity to sin. That's why God sent His Son. Jesus did for us what God requires from us. Jesus obeyed God for us, and we depend on His righteousness to make us right before God. Salvation is a gift given to us by God Himself. God provided for us His Son who did what we could not do, and who then laid down His life as an atoning sacrifice for our sins so we could be brought into a relationship with God.

When you trust in what Christ has done for you, your natural response will be a desire to live a life that honors God. You will want to obey God as an act of gratitude and worship. However, you still struggle with sin even after you trust Christ as Lord. You need God's help in order to obey Him, and God has given you help. His Holy Spirit lives within you and empowers you to live out God's desires. This does not mean obedience is easy, and it does not mean that you will obey God perfectly. However, it does mean God will help you. Anytime you ask for God to help you to live out what He desires for you, He will help you. He has given you His Spirit who will help you to live for your Father.

Think about what we said in the first chapter. The Disciple's Prayer is centered on God and not on us. When our lives are focused on living for our Father as a thankful and worshipful response to His adoption, our utmost desire is not bigger houses, bigger cars, and a better life on earth. Rather, our utmost desire is to do our Father's will. Our desire to do His will changes the way we pray and what we ask from God. We go from praying selfish prayers to asking God to help us accomplish whatever it is He desires from us.

Because God is your Father, you can ask Him for His help anytime you desire. You do not have to worry about waking Him up. You do not need to make an appointment. You do not need to go through His secretary. God is your Father. Anytime you need to ask Him for help, just ask.

I have two boys, and they always want stuff! Every time we take a trip to the store, I hear questions like, "Daddy, can I have that?" When I hear my boys ask that questions, sometimes I respond with yes, but many times I respond with no. Right now, when my oldest son asks me if he can have an iPhone, I have no problem telling him no. Someday when one of my sons asks me for a new car, I will tell him no. I will not answer all the requests my sons make according to their desires.

However, there are requests that I will always answer with a yes. When my boys ask me to pray with them, I will always do it. When my boys ask me to read them stories from the Bible, I find the time to read to them. When my boys ask me for counsel as to how to deal with a certain situation, I'm going to share my wisdom with them. When my boys ask me simply to spend time with them, I find a way to make it happen. Why? Those kinds of request are according to my will for them. I do not want to simply give my boys stuff for the sake of giving them stuff. Rather, I want to give them what I know they need to become the men God wants them to be. The more Luke and Hudson see that I want what's best for them, the better they will know how to make requests of me.

Luke and Hudson are my children, and all of my resources are available to them. My home is available for them to live in. My money is available to them. I would not give them a blank check or a credit card, but my money is used to provide them with meals to eat, clothes to wear, and an education. My knowledge and wisdom are available to them. They can seek my counsel, and I will give it to them. My love is available to them. I do not have a lot in this life, but what I do have is fully available to my sons. If they live according to my will, they are free to enjoy my resources. However, my boys enjoy my resources on my terms. They enjoy my resources as I determine. I am their father, and I choose what is best for them. I am wiser than they are. I know what they need better than they do. They have no right to demand that I give to them on their terms.

In a similar way, all of God's resources are available to you, and God gives His resources to you as He desires. His wisdom is available to you. His power is available to you. His love is available to you. His fellowship is available to you. His peace is available to you. His boldness is available to you. Because God is your Father you are free to ask Him to share His resources with you, and because God knows what is best for you, He will gladly give you His resources so you can accomplish what He desires for your life. This is the beauty of God being your Father. If He was just a Creator, King, or Judge you would have no right to ask Him for the use of His resources.

God knows His desires for you, and He knows how He wants to grow you to be like His Son, Jesus. The more you spend time with Him and enjoy your relationship with Him, the more you will ask Him for things that will help you to live out His desires for you. You can be sure that when you ask God to help you live out His desires for you, He will help you every time. God knows how to give you what is best for you, and what will cause you to live a life that will bring Him glory and honor. You have His listening ear. You can come to Him anytime you like knowing He will not turn you away. He will always listen to His children, and He always wants what is best for you.

I challenge you to spend uninterrupted time with God each day, and as you spend time with Him focus on what it means that He is your Father. Talk to Him as you would talk to your earthly father. God desires to give to you. What will you ask of Him?

7. *Can you find other passages of Scriptures in which Jesus teaches us to make requests of our Father? What do you think Jesus is teaching us about making requests of the Father in these other passages?*

8. *What kinds of requests can you make of God that you know He will answer positively?*

9. *How will knowing that your Father has a listening ear change the way that you pray?*

[3]

Hallowing God's Name

A Distinct Name

WE HAVE A FATHER, and as we already discussed, all He has is ours. Untold riches are at our disposal, but we must never forget our Father's unique identity. He is our Father in heaven who is perfect in every way, and He reigns and rules over the entire universe. He has a name that is above all names, and His name is worthy of all praise and adoration. Every time we pray to our Father, we should hallow His name. Do you see the contrast? In one breath Jesus tells us that we have a Father who loves us and desires intimacy with us, and in His next breath Jesus tells us that we better not forget that our Father is absolutely holy.

Often, when a father and mother named their child in biblical times that name had a significant meaning. I remember when Staci and I were trying to decide on a name for Luke. We were on the road to New Orleans to visit her parents, and as we rode in the car for ten hours, Staci sat with a pen and legal pad. We brainstormed all the possible names that came to mind. She circled the names we liked, and over and over again, reorganized our list. We knew we did not want our son to carry my full name. I am a junior, and we did not want a third! However, we did want our son to carry my first name, Thomas, as his middle name. We sounded out what seemed like hundreds of names with Thomas as the middle name to see what sounded best. Ultimately, we landed on Luke, and it stuck. Honestly, there was nothing significant about the name Luke. No one in our family is named Luke, so our son is not a namesake, and we did not name him Luke because of our love for Star Wars. (However, from time to time it does seem like he is playing some Jedi mind tricks on us.) We chose his name simply because we liked the way it sounded.

This was not necessarily the case in the Bible, especially in the Old Testament. Parents often chose names because of a name's meaning rather than the name's sound. Let me give you some examples. When Sarah, Abraham's wife, finally gave birth to a son in her old age she named him Isaac, which means *child of laughter*. In Genesis 18, God appeared as a man, along with two other men, to Abraham and Sarah. In this divine encounter God told Abraham that Sarah would have a son within a year. Sarah overheard and laughed to herself as she pondered the impossibility of having a child in her old age. You can imagine that her laughs of doubt turned to laughs of joy when Isaac was born.

Isaac eventually married Rebekah, and they had twins. The first boy was born with a body full of red hair, so they named him Esau, which probably means *hairy one*. The second son came out of his mother's womb holding on to Esau's heel, so they named him Jacob, which means *heel catcher* (Genesis 25:24-26). The Old Testament name *Moses* means *drawn out of water*, and the Old Testament name *Joshua*, which is translated as *Jesus* in the Greek New Testament, means *Yahweh is salvation*. In the New Testament, Jesus changed Simon's name to Peter, which means *rock*. These are just a few of numerous examples of names in the Bible that carried meaning based on something significant about that person.

The most significant name in the Bible is God's name. God's name describes the very essence of who He is. In Exodus 3, God revealed Himself to Moses in a burning bush, but the bush was not consumed by the fire. From the burning bush God spoke to Moses and told him to go before Pharaoh and demand that Pharaoh let the Hebrew slaves go free. Moses immediately questioned God. Why in the world would Pharaoh listen to Moses? Moses had killed an Egyptian and fled to the backwoods of Midian. Moses would be putting his life on the line even to go back to Egypt, and what in the world would Pharaoh think if this fugitive marched into his presence and demanded freedom for the Hebrew people? Pharaoh would likely laugh in his face and then behead him. For that matter, why would the Hebrews listen to Moses? Why would they believe he was God's appointed leader? He didn't even grow up among them. He grew up in Pharaoh's house and lived the life of luxury while his kinsmen were tortured at the hands of the Egyptians.

God assured Moses that He would be with him. There was no need for Moses to worry, but Moses was worried. He questioned God, "What is your name? Who am I going to say sent me? How are your own people going to know that I am for them if I don't know your name?" God told Moses His name: *I am who I am* (Exodus 3:14). That's an unusual name.

While it may seem like an unusual name, *I am who I am* describes God perfectly. If you remember English grammar, *am* is a state of being verb. When you see a being verb like *am*, *is*, or *are*, you expect information about the subject (in this case God) to follow. For example, I am male. Male is my state of being. Male is a descriptive word that describes what kind of person I always am. I could say other things about myself as well that would describe me, but eventually I would run out of ways to describe myself. However, you cannot run out of ways to describe God.

God says, "I am who I am." When God revealed His name to Moses He did not give Moses a descriptive word that explained who He was. God simply said, "I am who I am," or "I am God." God's name is so mysterious because the human vocabulary is not vast enough to describe an infinite God. You cannot put any information after the being verb *am* that adequately or completely describes who God is. Try it. God is holy. However, you cannot stop there. God is love. You cannot stop there either. God is infinite. You have to keep going. God is eternal. I could fill page after page with different descriptors of God, but while each page of descriptors might be true, all of those descriptors would not adequately describe the greatness of God. He is simply too powerful, too majestic, and too infinitely eternal for us to comprehend. To say that God's name is great is an understatement. God is simply the God who is, and this reality would have given Moses great comfort. As Moses went into the presence of Pharaoh, what fueled his confidence was the fact that the Great I Am was with Him. The One who is all powerful, almighty, all knowing, all wise, and infinitely good was on Moses' side, and He would deliver the Hebrew people just as He promised.

God's name, *I am who I am*, is seen throughout the Old Testament, but in our English Bibles, God's name is not translated each time it is used as *I am who I am*. When you read through the Old Testament of your Bible, you are likely to come across God's name translated as THE LORD in all capital letters. What is translated as THE LORD in our English Bibles is a form of the Hebrew word that means *I am who I am*. It is the Hebrew word *Yahweh*. God's name, *Yahweh*, became so sacred to the Jewish people that they would not say it out loud.

Another name in the Bible used to describe God is the Hebrew word *adonai*. The term *adonai*, which means *lord*, is a more generic word used to describe God. The term *adonai* is not reserved for God alone. Some humans might be called *lord*. A slave might call his master *lord*, or a subject of a kingdom might call the king *lord*. Since the Jews wanted there to be no confusion as to whom they were referring when they referenced God, and since they also viewed God's name as so holy that they did not want to say it, they combined the consonant sounds of *Yahweh* with the vowel sounds of *adonai* which formed the word *Jehovah*. When a Jew said *Jehovah*, other Jews knew exactly who they were talking about without saying the sacred name of God. While the early Jews disobeyed God repeatedly, and ultimately missed the Messiah, they certainly held the name of God in much higher regard than many of us who have embraced the Messiah and claim that He is our Lord.

I am not saying we should avoid saying the name of God. He is our Father. We have an intimate relationship with Him. We know His name, and we should share the greatness of His name with those who do not know Him. We should speak His name often. However, I think our modern Christian culture has lost much reverence for the name of God. We have forgotten that God is the God who is. He is the God who words cannot adequately describe. He is the God who is great, powerful, and mysterious. He is the God who on the one hand is our loving Father, but on the other hand is the God whose name is so holy that we should use his name very carefully.

You are well aware of how we use God's name so flippantly. In our own homes, many of us who profess faith in Christ, use the name of our God as a slang or curse word. We let our children watch mindless television shows that repeatedly curse God's name. We carelessly use the acronym OMG on Facebook. Isn't it interesting that typically we are not at all offended when we hear God's name belittled or disrespected? If someone were to talk badly about our spouses or our children we would be quick to defend their honor, but if we hear someone using our heavenly Father's name in a way that degrades who God is, we turn a deaf ear. Even worse, we degrade God ourselves by flippantly using His great name as a slang word.

Every time you use God's name as a curse word or write OMG on a Facebook post or text message, you are taking God's name in vain. You are breaking the fourth commandment, and you are belittling the greatness of our God who sent His Son to die on the cross for you. Let us be very careful never to take the name of God lightly. Let us treat Him with the honor and reverence He is due. Consider what D. Martyn Lloyd Jones said about the name of God.

> What unworthy ideas and notions this world has of God! If you test your ideas of God by the teaching of the Scriptures you will see at a glance what I mean. We lack even a due sense of the greatness and the might and the majesty of God. Listen to men arguing about God, and notice how glibly they use the term … It is indeed almost alarming to observe the way in which we all tend to use the name of God. We obviously do not realize that we are talking about the ever blessed, eternal, and absolute, almighty God. There is a sense in which we should take our shoes off our feet whenever we use the name [1]

1. If you were to describe God to someone, how could you describe Him in a way that captures the essence of His name?

2. In what ways does God's name bring you comfort?

3. Why do you think so many Christians take God's name so lightly?

4. When you hear someone use God's name in vain, how does it affect you?

A Distinct Name Worthy of Praise

In the Disciple's Prayer, Jesus is calling us to remember how great God's name is by instructing us to hallow God's name. When was the last time you used the word *hallow*? To hallow something means to treat it as sacred or holy. To hallow something is to set that thing apart from everything else and put it in a place of primary importance. Therefore, to hallow God's name is to set Him apart from everything else in the universe and put Him in a place of primary importance in your life. The phrase, "hallowed be your name," is not a phrase you can utter as a meaningless ritual. This is a call to worship God and acknowledge Him for who He is.

How do you know if you hallow God's name? How do you know if He is of primary importance to you? Examine the way you pray. If God is of primary importance to you, your prayers will be upward before they are inward. Let me explain what I mean. When you pray upward prayers your focus is on exalting God and making much of His great name. Inward prayers are more focused on what you can get from God rather than giving Him the praise He is due. When your prayers are upward you will think of who God is and what He has done for you before you think of yourself and what you need.

How do you approach God when you pray? Do you approach Him with a sense of gratitude for what He has done for you? Do you thank God for the salvation He has given you through Jesus? Do you approach Him with a sense of awe for who He is? Do you approach Him with humility knowing the only reason you are allowed in His presence is because of His grace that He demonstrated to you through the death of His own Son? Do you approach God with a sense of dependency knowing you can do nothing apart from His power at work within you? If this is how you approach God, you are praying upward prayers. You are approaching Him in worship. You are hallowing His name.

When you pray, are your prayers simply a list of actions you would like God to perform on your behalf? Or, do you ignore God by not praying at all? You might profess Christianity, but maybe you live as if God exists only on Sunday morning. The rest of your week is spent indulging in your own self-sufficiency. You have your own life figured out, and you think you have no need for God to be involved in the daily details of your life. Sure, you pray, but you pray only when you need something. When tragedy strikes or when there is an issue in your life that is too big for you to handle, you turn to God, but when things are going well, God is a mere afterthought. If this is you, you do not hallow God's name. He is not of primary importance to you. Rather, you are of primary importance to you. You hallow your own name, not God's name.

The Pharisees are the prime example of people who did not hallow God's name. Instead, they hallowed their own names. We briefly saw in chapter one that Jesus taught His followers not to pray like the Pharisees (Matthew 6:5). The Pharisees wanted attention. They wanted to be known for their zeal for the Lord. Each day in Jerusalem the priests offered sacrifices in the morning and afternoon, and when the priests offered the sacrifices trumpets would blow. The sounding of the trumpets signaled it was time for people to pause and pray. The Pharisees timed it just right. They positioned themselves on the busiest street corners in Jerusalem, and when they heard the trumpet, they turned toward the temple, lifted their hands and prayed as loudly as they could to make sure everyone could hear them. According to Jesus, the Pharisees were nothing more than actors. Their lives were inconsistent. On the outside they looked extremely spiritual, but on the inside their hearts were dead. Simply put, they wanted their will to be done more than God's will to be done, and their will was that others would notice them for their religious zeal. In Matthew 23:27, Jesus said to the Pharisees,

> Woe to you, scribes and Pharisees, hypocrites! For you are like whitewashed tombs, which outwardly appear beautiful, but within are full of dead people's bones and all uncleanness.

The Pharisees were not as much interested in helping others hallow the name of God as they were hallowing their own names. Jesus said they had received their reward. They got exactly what they wanted: recognition from others.

Now, you are probably thinking, "I am nothing like the Pharisees." In a sense, you are probably right. I have yet to see anyone in our congregation standing on a street corner, facing a church, lifting hands, and shouting to God. We might not be as outwardly zealous about our spirituality being seen publicly as the Pharisees were, but we are often just as inwardly zealous about hallowing our own name. We desperately want to see our will done, and if we say we are Christ-followers while inwardly wanting our will to be done over God's will, we're just as hypocritical as the Pharisees.

Be honest. You are not much different than the Pharisees. You often place yourself at the center of your life, and when you do, you'd rather people notice you than the God who lives within you. Isn't it true that many of the decisions we make on a daily basis are based on how those decisions will promote what we want and what others think of us? Maybe you choose your clothing each morning with the hopes that others will praise you for your attractiveness. Maybe you work hard at your job with the hopes that your boss or peers will notice your hard work and praise you for it. Maybe you push your children to be the best students or athletes they can be so you will be praised for being a wonderful parent. Maybe you have purchased an elaborate home, vehicle, and the best in designer goods so you might appear successful and be praised for your accomplishments. If you looked at your motivation for the things you do, you might be surprised to find you hallow your name above God's name.

We are more like the Pharisees than we would like to admit. If you ever find yourself seeking your praise above God's praise, you are a hypocrite. Hypocrites are inconsistent. A hypocrite will be quick to say, "I praise God, and I live for Him," but a hypocrite's life will demonstrate that he is primarily concerned about himself. A hypocrite will gather for worship on Sunday morning with a smile on his face and lift his hands in worship, but on Monday morning, a hypocrite will lie and cheat in order to get the promotion he so desperately wants. A hypocrite will have all the right answers in a small group Bible study, but after Bible study she will be quick to gossip on the phone with her girlfriends about others in an attempt to make herself look better than the people she is gossiping about. You and I are actors who put on a good show. We say and do all the right Christian things in hopes that others will applaud us for our outstanding Christian performance.

We are all hypocrites. Maybe our issue is not praying as loudly as we can in public so others can see our spirituality, but we all have inconsistencies in our walk with the Lord. Our inconsistencies tend to show up in the way we pray. When our prayers are inward rather than upward we make requests like, "Lord, please help me out of this mess I'm in," or, "I could really use a raise at work. Please convince my boss to give me a raise." It's almost as if we treat God as our celestial Santa Claus who exists simply to give us what we want.

Inward prayers demonstrate that what we are after is not knowing and doing the will of God but rather seeking our own will. If we are not careful our prayers can be nothing more than, "Lord, do according to my will so my life won't be too difficult and so others will notice how good I am." These kinds of inward prayers demonstrate our desire for God to hallow our name rather than a desire to hallow His name.

We have already seen that God does desire to give His children good gifts, and it is not wrong to make requests of God. However, making requests of God should always flow out of a heart that wants His will more than our own will. This is why the Disciple's Prayer is primarily focused on God and not on man. Jesus focuses us on God's holiness to expose our hypocritical tendencies and to show us that God is far more than our celestial Santa Claus.

How do we change our hypocritical ways? How do we move from being a people whose prayers are self-centered to being a people whose prayers are focused on adoring and praising our God? It starts by getting alone with God, reflecting on who He is, and praising God for who He is. Jesus told His followers in Matthew 6:6, "But when you pray, go into your room and shut the door and pray to your Father who is in secret." Jesus is not teaching us never to pray in public. Rather, He is teaching us that if we want to learn to pray in such a way that God's will, rather than our own will, is at the center of our prayers, we must get alone with Him.

What are you supposed to do when you are alone with God? First, repent of your tendency to glorify yourself instead of glorifying God. James 4:8 says, "Draw near to God, and he will draw near to you. Cleanse your hands, you sinners, and purify your hearts, you double-minded." Second, reflect on God's greatness and the salvation He has given you and praise Him for it. I find it most helpful to pray with an open Bible. If you are just starting to learn to pray in a way that hallows God's name rather than yours, I suggest you pray with your Bible open to the Book of Psalms. The psalmists write in a way that stirs your heart to honor the God of all creation. The Book of Psalms can be a great help to you as you hallow and adore God's name in your prayer time. For example, consider Psalm 146:

> Praise the Lord! Praise the Lord, O my soul! I will praise the Lord as long as I live; I will sing praises to my God while I have my being. Put not your trust in princes, in a son of man, in whom there is no salvation. When his breath departs, he returns to the earth; on that very day his plans perish. Blessed is he whose help is the God of Jacob, whose hope is in the Lord his God, who made heaven and earth, the sea, and all that is in them, who keeps faith forever; who executes justice for the oppressed, who gives food to the hungry. The Lord sets the prisoners free; the Lord opens the eyes of the blind. The Lord lifts up those who are bowed down; the Lord loves the righteous. The Lord watches over the sojourners; he upholds the widow and the fatherless, but the way of the wicked he brings to ruin.

You can take a psalm like this and simply repeat to God the content of this psalm in your own words as a prayer to Him. This has two advantages. On one hand, praying Scripture to God will always teach you about the character of God as you meditate on His Word. On the other hand, praying Scripture will always fuel your prayers. Think about how you might pray through Psalm 146. You might say something like this to the Lord:

> *Lord I praise you because you are great and mighty. Help me to see your greatness and give me a desire to praise you as long as I live. I praise you that I do not have to put all of my trust in sinful men. Rather, I can place all of my trust in you because you are always faithful. You are forever faithful, and you are forever just. There are many in this world who are hurting and oppressed, and I praise you that when the hurting and oppressed look to you they find freedom. I thank you that you give freedom to those searching for freedom and that you are a Father to those who need a father. You will always reign, and I ask you to help me submit to your reign.*

Using the Psalms, or other passages in Scripture that point to the greatness of God, is a great way to help you understand the greatness of God and center your prayers round His greatness. The more you get in the habit of adoring God's name in your prayers, the more you will desire to conform your will to God's will rather than trying to conform God's will to your will. When you have a heart of gratitude for all God has done for you, you cannot help but to hallow His name with humble adoration. Praise naturally flows from a thankful heart. If there is a praise problem, the root of your praise problem is probably an ungrateful heart. If your heart is ungrateful, continually go back to the Gospel. Remember who you were before you came to Christ and who you are now in Christ. If going back to the Gospel does not make you eternally grateful to the God of all creation, you might not really know Him.

5. *Examine the way you pray. Do your prayers typically start with hallowing God's name?*

6. *How do you think hallowing God's name would change the way that you pray?*

7. *What do you think keeps believers from having a heart that overflows with gratitude towards God?*

8. *Dig into God's Word. What are some Psalms and other passages of Scripture that can help you to hallow God's name?*

A Distinct Name to Imitate

I have always wondered what it would be like to be the child of someone famous and powerful. I come from a normal family of humble means. While my mom and dad were leaders in our church as I was growing up, their fame certainly did not spread throughout the community. My dad works at a plant, and my mom is a nurse. Outside of their respective places of business, they simply are not that well known. My parents have never served on the city council. They have never run a Fortune 500 company. They have never played professional sports or starred in a Hollywood blockbuster. My family lives in relative obscurity, and that's the way we like it. It's not that way for everyone though. Can you imagine what it must be like, for example, to be the child of the President or a famous athlete or movie star? All eyes are on you because of who your parents' fame. When we look at the President's children, we wonder how they will turn out. Will they be like their dad? Will they find the same political success? Or, we look at the child of a professional athlete and wonder if he will have the same athletic ability as his father. All eyes are on the child of a celebrity to see how he or she will imitate his or her parents.

Your Father is not the President, nor is your Father a movie star or a star quarterback in the NFL. Your Father is infinitely greater and infinitely more powerful, and you can rest assured when you claim you are a child of the God of all creation, all eyes are on you. People will wonder if you will live as if you belong to the Father you claim to have. This is why Paul says in Ephesians 5:1,

> Therefore be imitators of God, as beloved children. And walk in love, as Christ loved us and gave himself up for us, a fragrant offering and sacrifice to God.

We do not imitate God by taking His glory for ourselves. God's glory and fame belong to Him alone. We cannot steal His glory. We're not like the son of a professional who wants to surpass the success of his father. We will never surpass our heavenly Father. He will always be greater than us. He will always be God, and we will never be God.

We imitate God by living lives that are set apart. Imitating God means we strive for holiness in our daily walk with the Lord. We seek, with the Holy Spirit's help, to crucify the flesh, die to our desires, and live for His desires. We seek to be honest, just, and true to our word. If you read Scripture carefully you will discover how to live a life that honors the Lord. By living a life that imitates our Lord, you will not steal His glory. Rather, you will point people to His glory. God's will is that people from every tribe, tongue, and nation will hallow His name. The greater His name is to us, the more we will desire to live for His great name and point people to Him.

Sadly, we live in a Christian culture in which nominal Christianity rules the day. I know many people who claim God as their Father, but their lives do not demonstrate that they have a relationship with the Father at all. Immerse yourself in the greatness of God. Learn to delight in hallowing His name so you will desire to live in thankful obedience to Him. As you live in thankful obedience you will be a Gospel witness who points others to Him. Do not underestimate the Gospel influence you can have on others as you daily live out what it means to hallow God's name.

9. *How does hallowing God's name challenge you to live for Him?*

10. *How will you hallow God's name in your prayer life this week? What will be your plan of action?*

[4]

Longing for a Kingdom

GOD IS OUR HEAVENLY FATHER who delights in His children, but our Father is also a great king who is worthy of our allegiance and full obedience. God is king right now. Psalm 24:1 says, "The earth is the Lord's and the fullness thereof, the world and those who dwell therein..." Psalm 99:1-2 says, "The Lord reigns; let the peoples tremble! He sits enthroned upon the cherubim; let the earth quake! The Lord is great in Zion; he is exalted over all the peoples." Your Father is a mighty king, and no one can remove Him from His throne.

This is good news for us because we live in a world in which it seems God is not reigning and ruling. It seems that injustice is everywhere. Just recently I watched a documentary on North Korea. I knew the people of North Korea were oppressed, but I never realized just how much control the North Korean dictator has over his people. In the documentary, the North Korean government, under the leadership of

Kim Jong-il, allowed an ophthalmologist to enter the country and perform cataract surgery on a number of patients. This doctor literally did hundreds of surgeries over the course of a little over a week.

At the end of his time in the country, many of the patients gathered in a room together and one by one their bandages were taken off. The response was the same for each patient. For the first time in years, the patients could see clearly, and one by one each patient stood up and walked to the front of the room where a huge portrait of Jong-il hung. Each patient approached the portrait and gave Jong-il thanks for their renewed sight. Jong-il had done absolutely nothing good for these eye patients. Rather, he had oppressed them for years, but in spite of his oppression, the people worshipped him as a god! Jong-il has since met the Lord face to face, and he has seen once and for all that there is only one King who sits on a throne and is worthy of worship!

While the evil dictators of the world set themselves up as gods and reject the rule of the Ultimate King, ordinary people also reject the rule of God. Sadly, even God's own people have a tendency to reject His rule. In the Old Testament the Israelites were not satisfied with God's rule. God blessed them beyond imagination, but the Israelites treated His goodness with contempt. They decided they did not need his rule. The Israelites wrongly assumed a human king, like the other nations had, was what they needed.

> Then all the elders of Israel gathered together and came to Samuel at Ramah and said to him, "Behold, you are old

and your sons do not walk in your ways. Now appoint for us a king to judge us like all the nations." But the thing displeased Samuel when they said, "Give us a king to judge us." And Samuel prayed to the Lord. And the Lord said to Samuel, "Obey the voice of the people in all that they say to you, for they have not rejected you, but they have rejected me from being king over them. According to all the deeds that they have done, from the day I brought them up out of Egypt even to this day, forsaking me and serving other gods, so they are also doing to you. Now then, obey their voice; only you shall solemnly warn them and show them the ways of the king who shall reign over them." (1 Samuel 8:4-9)

Let's be honest. We're not much different than the Israelites. Even as God's own people who have been saved through faith in Jesus Christ we have a tendency to reject God's rule from time to time. We want a Savior who saves us from eternal hell, but we don't often want a king who governs over our lives. We would rather govern our own lives. Therefore, to pray, "your kingdom come" is to pray a radical prayer of surrender.

1. *What does it mean that God is King?*

2. *How is the kingship of God reflected in your own life?*

Let Your Reign Be Established in Me

Jesus spoke often about the kingdom of God. Shortly after Jesus' temptation in the wilderness he began preaching about the kingdom of God. Matthew writes, "From that time Jesus began to preach, saying, 'Repent, for the kingdom of heaven is at hand'" (Matthew 4:17). Jesus said in Luke 4:43, "I must preach the good news of the kingdom of God to the other towns as well; for I was sent for this purpose." According to Kent Hughes, the kingdom of God is mentioned 103 times in Matthew, Mark, and Luke.[1] It's obvious that Jesus was passionate about the kingdom of God.

When you think of a kingdom you probably think of a specific people in a specific location at a specific time in history. Perhaps the most media-covered monarchy is the British monarchy. Or, maybe you think of Camelot and King Arthur. Perhaps you think of some fairy tale with a kind and benevolent king who rules over his land. Regardless, when you think of a kingdom, you think of a king ruling over a specific group of people at a specific time in history in a specific place. However, when Jesus spoke of the kingdom of God he was not speaking of a physical place, a specific people, or a specific period of time.

What did Jesus mean when He spoke of the kingdom of God? Perhaps J.I. Packer describes the kingdom of God best. In his book, *Growing in Christ*, Packer writes,

> God's kingdom is not a place, but rather a relationship. It exists wherever people enthrone Jesus as lord of their lives.[2]

Anyone can be a part of God's kingdom through faith in Christ, and God's kingdom is full of righteousness, peace, and joy. Paul writes in Romans 14:17, "For the kingdom of God is not a matter of eating and drinking but of righteousness and peace and joy in the Holy Spirit."

Think about what Paul writes. God's kingdom is unlike any other kingdom on this earth. In God's kingdom you can expect perfect righteousness. In other words, God will never make a bad decision. Can you imagine that? We frequently criticize our national leaders for the poor decisions they make, but God never makes a poor decision! God is perfect, and He will always make perfect decisions. God is always good as well, and His decisions will always be for the good of His children. In His kingdom you can expect perfect peace. In this world peace is hard to come by, and even Christians struggle to live at peace. We have an enemy who is raging war against us, and the battle is tough. However, you can have peace in the midst of the battle because you know you already have ultimate victory. In Christ, your eternal destiny is sealed. You will come through this life in complete victory, and you will enjoy eternity with the Father. Satan's destiny is sealed as well. When Christ comes again, Satan will be cast into the lake of fire never to assault you again. You can have peace even when the battle rages because your victory is certain. In God's kingdom you can expect pure joy. Your heart longs for joy. You long for deep satisfaction and contentment, and you find the satisfaction you long for only in God's kingdom.

Jesus told the Pharisees in Luke 17:21, "Behold, the kingdom of God is in the midst of you." In essence, Jesus was saying, "Look! I'm here! I am the kingdom of God! I've come to bring you into a lasting kingdom full of righteousness, peace, and joy through my death and resurrection." The Pharisees did not believe it, and neither do we apart from the saving work of Jesus Christ. Instead of believing that the kingdom of God is the source of everything that is soul-satisfying, we believe we can establish our own kingdoms on this earth in which we rule. We believe we can find our own satisfaction apart from God. The kingdom of this earth is our attempt to rule and reign over our lives apart from the Lordship of Christ. It is our attempt to establish our own kingdom, but if you think you can rule and reign over your life, you have bought the lie of Satan.

Whenever you try to control your own life you have given in to the influence of Satan. In the Book of Revelation, John describes Satan as a dragon who makes war on those who keep the commandments of God and hold to the testimony of Jesus (Revelation 12:17). Satan daily attacks you, and one of the ways he attacks is through his lies. Jesus called Satan the father of all lies (John 8:44), and Satan lies to you by convincing you to believe you are perfectly able to rule over your own life without the help of God. If you are in Christ, you know better. Do not believe the lie.

In Ephesians 2:1-2 (which we referenced in chapter 3), Paul writes to a group of believers who had recently converted to the Christian faith, and he reminds them that before they came to Christ, they allowed Satanic influence to dominate their lives. Paul writes,

> And you were dead in the trespasses and sins in which you once walked, following the course of this world, following the prince of the power of the air, the spirit that is now at work in the sons of disobedience...

Satan has set himself up as the ruler of the world, and he attempts to enslave humanity to his influence, but if you have trusted Christ, Satan is not your master. You have been transferred from Satan's kingdom of darkness to the eternal kingdom of God. Paul writes,

> He has delivered us from the domain of darkness and transferred us to the kingdom of his beloved Son, in whom we have redemption, the forgiveness of sins. (Colossians 1:13-14)

If you are of the kingdom of God in which Jesus is the perfect ruler, why would you go back to believing Satan's lie that you can do a better job of ruling over your life than God can do? You do not have to give in to Satan's influence. As a believer, when you take control of your life out of God's hands and place it in your hands, you are doing exactly what Satan wants you to do. You are allowing him to influence you rather than allowing the Spirit of God control you.

Jesus has saved you so you might know He is a far better ruler than you or Satan will ever be. If you are not a follower of Christ, please know Satan does not have your best interest at heart. Do not believe his lies. In John 10:10, Jesus said, "The thief comes only to steal and kill and destroy. I came that they may have life and have it abundantly." You are going to submit to the rule of Satan or you are going to submit to the rule of Jesus. Satan knows his destiny. He knows he will be destroyed, and as he looks toward his own defeat he desires that many be defeated along with him. Satan wants to take you down with him. Jesus, on the other hand, wants to give you abundant life: a life of righteousness, joy, and peace. Wouldn't it make sense to submit to the true King and to allow Him to rule over your life? If you are a believer who has been transferred to God's kingdom, why would you want to go back to your former way of life in which you tried to call the shots of your own life? Why would you take control of your life back from God and open yourself up to the influence of the enemy?

If you are a follower of Christ, never lose sight of the reality that God's kingdom is the only kingdom in which you are guaranteed victory and life everlasting. Make seeking God's kingdom the priority of your life. You do not experience the blessings of God's kingdom by rejecting His rule, nor do you experience the blessings of God's kingdom by living apathetically towards Him. Jesus said in Matthew 6:33, "But seek first the kingdom of God and his righteousness, and all these things will be added to you." How do you seek God's kingdom? You begin by falling on your face and praying in absolute surrender knowing that apart from the Holy Spirit's help you will always have a tendency to settle for the kingdom of this earth and its empty promises. You need the

Holy Spirit to remind you constantly that God's kingdom is better, eternal, and soul-satisfying.

Do you daily surrender to the Lordship of Christ? Daily surrender really is the key to the victorious Christian life. We only gain the life that Christ has for us when lose our lives. Jesus said in Luke 9:24, "For whoever would save his life will lose it, but whoever loses his life for my sake will save it." When we give Christ daily control of our lives, we find real purposeful life. Yet daily surrender is what we struggle with most. While we have been gloriously saved, we still battle with our sinful flesh that continually resists the work of God within us. A battle rages within you, and you must daily surrender if you are going to experience the abundant life God has for you. Daily pray:

> *I give up. I am powerless, and when I take my eyes off of you, I always find myself settling for the kingdom of this earth. I need you to rule over me. I need you to make my decisions for me. I need you to order my steps, because when I make my own decisions and order my own steps, it always leads me farther away from you rather than closer to you. I surrender. I give up. You and you alone know what's best for my life, and I give you complete control to do in my life as you desire.*

That is a prayer of surrender. When you begin to ask God daily to reign and rule over your own life, you will begin to experience righteousness, peace, and joy. The blessings of God's kingdom overflow in your life only as you submit to His rule. Are you willing to pray this radical prayer of surrender?

3. What are the benefits of belonging to the kingdom of God?

4. Is it possible to be a child of God and not allow Him to reign and rule in your life?

5. What keeps you from daily surrendering to God's reign and rule in your life? Do you desire His reign and rule? Why or why not?

6. What would your local church look like if your church was fully surrendered to the reign and rule of God? What can your church do now to submit to the reign and rule of Christ?

LET YOUR REIGN EXTEND THROUGHOUT THE EARTH

Once you've experienced the joy of letting God reign in your own life, you desire to see God's reign extended throughout the earth. You desire to see your family experience the same joy you experience in Christ. You long for your friends to know the same Prince of Peace you know. You even long for people you don't know to experience the righteousness of God that you've experienced. When the kingdom of God is established in your own life, you realize how desperately the kingdom of God needs to be established throughout the earth. Praying for God's kingdom to come is not only an individual prayer of radical surrender, this is also a prayer begging God to advance His kingdom throughout the world.

God advances His kingdom throughout the world through the faithful Gospel witness of the Church. God's plan to extend His reign throughout the earth is to raise up His Church to proclaim to a world entranced by Satan that there is a better king who gives eternal righteousness, peace, and joy. Right before Jesus sent seventy-two of His disciples out to spread the message of the kingdom of God, He told them to pray for the advancement of the kingdom. What He told them to pray is quite interesting. Jesus said to His disciples,

> The harvest is plentiful, but the laborers are few. Therefore pray earnestly to the Lord of the harvest to send out laborers into his harvest. (Luke 10:2)

Did you notice that Jesus did not tell His followers to pray for the many lost people they would encounter? He didn't tell His followers to pray that the eyes of the lost might be opened spiritually to the Gospel, and He didn't tell His followers to ask God to draw lost people to Himself. I'm not saying, nor is Jesus, that we should not pray for people who are far away from Christ. We do not pray enough for people who are far away from Christ. We need to wrestle in prayer over family members, friends, and coworkers for their salvation. We need to pray not only for those in our immediate circle of relationships or in our community, but we need to pray for the darkness that penetrates the entire globe. We need to pray for lost people.

Jesus told His disciples to pray for workers to go into the field. Jesus knew the multitudes of lost people the disciples would encounter, and He knew there was a great harvest waiting. He knew many would respond positively to the message of God's kingdom. He knew people were longing for hope. Jesus also knew many would not respond positively to the message of the kingdom.

Jesus also knew His followers would face ridicule and persecution. Engaging a lost world meant engaging the enemy, and Jesus knew His followers would be hesitant to go into the battle. As soon as Jesus told His disciples to pray for workers to go into the field, He told them what kind of world they were going into. Jesus said in Luke 10:3, "Go your way; behold, I am sending you out as lambs in the midst of wolves." Wolves eat lambs, and throughout history, many

Christians have laid down their lives among the wolves making the Gospel known. Knowing we are like lambs among wolves doesn't diminish our responsibility to share the Gospel. Rather, knowing we are going out as lambs among wolves should drive us to our knees. We must pray for Gospel workers who will not succumb to fear and retreat, but who will rise up with boldness and in the power of God to obediently make Christ known even in the most difficult places.

Are you praying for the advancement of the kingdom of God, and are you praying for the church to rise up and declare the glory of the King to a lost world in spite of the inherit dangers? Think about the Christians who are close to you. Think about the members of your small group or Sunday School class. How often do you pray for them to make the most of their encounters with those who do not know Christ? Our churches are really good at composing long prayer lists. We will be quick to pray for a small group member who is going through a difficult time, or we will be quick to pray for a Sunday School classmate who is struggling with a terminal illness. Certainly, we should pray for the needs of others. We should pray for healing and other needs of our brothers and sisters in Christ. James 5:13-18 commands it. However, when was the last time you prayed for those you are closest to in the body of Christ to be effective in their Gospel witness? When was the last time you prayed by name for the people in your small group or Sunday School class to have an impact for Christ at their workplace or at their school?

If anyone knew the difficulties of engaging a hostile world, it was the early followers of Jesus in the Book of Acts.

They experienced intense persecution because of their faith. They were persecuted by their Jewish brethren who saw this new Christian movement as a threat to the Jewish faith. They also experienced persecution at the hands of the Roman Empire. In Acts 4, Peter and John, two apostles of Jesus, were arrested and brought before a Jewish council. Their destiny was in the hands of this council, but they preached the Gospel with boldness. They were set free, but their arrest and hearing before the council was a reminder to the early church that penetrating their community with the Gospel was not going to be easy. They were going out as lambs among wolves. Knowing persecution was before them, they did not retreat; they prayed as they anticipated even greater persecution.

> And now, Lord, look upon their threats and grant to your servants to continue to speak your word with all boldness, while you stretch out your hand to heal, and signs and wonders are performed through the name of your holy servant Jesus. (Acts 4:29-30)

I saw this kind of boldness on display on a trip I led to a country in East Asia several years ago. I led a group of American believers to work alongside believers in that country who are regularly persecuted because of their faith. During our time in East Asia we learned that two local believers we had met were getting ready to find a way into North Korea to advance the kingdom of God in that dangerous country. Can you imagine trying to sneak into the most dangerous country in the world in order to share the good news of Christ? These East Asian believers willingly put their lives on the line because they recognized the kingdom of God is much more valuable than their own lives. They realized that people in North Korea need to know there is a better king than the evil dictator who rules over North Korea. These East Asian believers are going out among the wolves to proclaim to the people of North Korea that the God of all creation is worthy of allegiance and worship. In our American congregations we have a hard time getting people to serve the Lord by ministering to children in our church nurseries. If we are not willing to serve the Lord in the comforts of a modern church facility, we're probably not going to be willing to go out among the wolves to declare the glory of our king.

The true follower of Christ longs to see the kingdom of God advanced throughout this world, and we know the Church is God's plan to advance His kingdom. However, we also know the task before us is not easy. We are going out as sheep among wolves. We need to pray for the advancement of His kingdom. We need to pray His reign will extend to the farthest parts of the world, and we need to pray that He will give us boldness to take the message of the kingdom wherever He leads us. Kingdom expansion begins on our knees. We must cry out to our God and ask Him to give us boldness to make His kingdom known.

How are you praying for kingdom advancement? How are you leading your family to pray for kingdom advancement? My wife is passionate about the global advancement of the Gospel. She served as an overseas missionary herself, so she still knows missionaries on the field. We pray for the global advancement of the kingdom by praying regularly for specific missionaries she knows. Staci also receives a monthly periodical produced by our denomination that each month gives the birthdays of missionaries serving on behalf of our denomination. In the mornings, as I am leaving for work, Staci will sit at the kitchen table with Luke and Hudson, and they will pray for missionaries, on their birthdays, who are striving to advance the kingdom in various parts of the world.

You can pray the same way. I would encourage you to begin by praying for your Christian friends. Pray for them to be effective witnesses of Jesus Christ among their family, in their work, and in the community, but also begin to pray for those serving in various parts of the world. Visit the International Mission Board website, imb.org. You will find a number of ways you can pray for the advancement of the kingdom. A resource that has been helpful for me has been the book *Operation World*. *Operation World* is a massive and well-researched book that lists every country in the world and the different spiritual needs of each country. The author also lists specific ways to pray for each country. If you follow the author's prayer plan, over the course of a year you will pray for kingdom advancement in each nation of the world. If you long to see the kingdom expanded throughout the world, kingdom expansion begins on your knees.

7. If you are studying this book with a group, pause right now and pray for each group member to be effective in his or her Gospel witness.

8. *Why is prayer so important in expanding the kingdom of God? How often do you pray for the expansion of His kingdom? How can you pray for the advancement of the kingdom within your local community and beyond your local community?*

9. *How might you lead your small group and your family to pray more effectively for the advancement of the kingdom?*

Let Your Reign be Unhindered

God's kingdom will advance through His faithful people who seek His kingdom first and pray for boldness to go out into the world as sheep among wolves. However, in this present age, the advancement of God's kingdom is hindered because this world is broken. Even among believers who have surrendered to God's rule, we allow our own sin to hinder His reign in our lives. You and I daily battle to submit to Christ's reign over our lives even though we know that allowing Christ to reign in our lives is best for us. Therefore, "your kingdom come" is also a call for us to pray for Christ to return to reign and rule perfectly over this world.

Can you imagine what it would be like if Jesus was physically here right now? Can you imagine what it would be like if everyone on the planet knew He was in charge and submitted to His rule? Do you think there would be any injustice? The Bible promises us a day is coming when every knee will bow, and every tongue will confess that Jesus is Lord (Philippians 2:9-11). We long for that day. Not only do we long for that day, but all of creation longs for the day that Christ will return, recreate this earth, and reign once and for all as the only King and only Lord. Paul wrote in Romans 8:22-23,

> For we know that the whole creation has been groaning together in the pains of childbirth until now. And not only the creation, but we ourselves, who have the firstfruits of the Spirit, groan inwardly as we wait eagerly for adoption as sons, the redemption of our bodies.

The Apostle John gives us a vivid picture of what it will be like one day when Christ returns and reigns as Lord once and for all. John wrote in Revelation 21:1-8:

> Then I saw a new heaven and a new earth, for the first heaven and the first earth had passed away, and the sea was no more. And I saw the holy city, new Jerusalem, coming down out of heaven from God, prepared as a bride adorned for her husband. And I heard a loud voice from the throne saying, "Behold, the dwelling place of God is with man. He will dwell with them, and they will be his people, and God himself will be with them as their God. He will wipe away every tear from their eyes, and death shall be no more, neither shall there be mourning, nor crying, nor pain anymore, for the former things have passed away." And he who was seated on the throne said, "Behold, I am making all things new." Also he said, "Write this down, for these words are trustworthy and true." And he said to me, "It is done! I am the Alpha and the Omega,

the beginning and the end. To the thirsty I will give from the spring of the water of life without payment. The one who conquers will have this heritage, and I will be his God and he will be my son. But as for the cowardly, the faithless, the detestable, as for murderers, the sexually immoral, sorcerers, idolaters, and all liars, their portion will be in the lake that burns with fire and sulfur, which is the second death.

When you read that passage of Scripture does it excite you? Can you imagine? A day is coming when everything will be new, and God's justice will be perfect and final. Think of the most beautiful sight you have ever seen on this earth. One day, it will be recreated, and it will be even more breathtaking because God's creation will one day be perfected and no longer affected by the fall of humanity. No longer will sin have any dominion whatsoever over this earth, and no longer will we suffer and mourn. Our God will dwell with us. We will see Him, and we will enjoy Him for all of eternity. God's kingdom will come once and for all, and no one will ever again compete with His rule.

Do you long for that day? Do you pray for Christ to return? One day He will come, and your prayer for His kingdom to come will be answered completely. Packer gives great advice on how to pray for God's kingdom to come. Carefully consider his words and make them your daily prayer.

> To pray "thy kingdom come" is searching and demanding, for one must be ready to add, "and start with me; make me your fully obedient subject. Show me my place among 'workers for the kingdom of God' (Colossians 4:11), and

use me, so far as may be, to extend the kingdom and so be your means of answering my prayer."[3]

10. Why should you pray for the return of Christ?

11. Why do you think we struggle to pray regularly for the return of Christ?

12. Spend time each day praying for God's kingdom to be established in your heart, in the hearts of those who are far from Him. Also, spend time reflecting on what it will be like when Christ returns. Let thoughts of Christ's return encourage you to pray for His coming.

[5]

Your Will Be Done

A Dangerous Petition

"Your will be done on earth as it is in heaven" is a dangerous petition to pray to God if you love your own comforts more than you love God. Praying this petition gives God permission to do whatever He desires in your life without your objections. This is how Jesus teaches us to pray, but are you willing to pray this way? Are you willing to say, "God, my life belongs to you, and just as nothing stops your will from being accomplished in heaven, I want nothing to stop your will from being done in my life"?

This was the prayer of Adoniram Judson. After learning about the work of William Carey, a missionary in India, Judson's eyes were opened to the need to take the Gospel to foreign lands. However, he struggled to find his place in God's divine plan to reach the nations. In his struggle, his prayer was, "More than all else, I long to please Thee, my Lord. What wilt Thou have me to do?"[1]

Judson began to gather with several young men to pray. During their times of prayer these young men made a commitment to take the Gospel to the nations. Eventually Judson, along with his wife Ann, left the states and arrived in Rangoon, Burma on July 13, 1813 to serve a people among whom there were no known believers. Burma was a hostile nation, and Carey told Judson not to go to Burma because of the hardships Judson was bound to experience.[2] Judson was convinced he was in the center of God's will, but just as Carey warned, Judson did experience tremendous hardship as he labored for the sake of the Gospel. Throughout his forty-year-ministry among the Burmese people, Judson and his family fought constant one-hundred-degree heat, cholera, malaria, dysentery, and other physical ailments. While serving in Burma his wife and seven of his thirteen children died of diseases that would have been preventable in a more modernized country. Judson also found himself imprisoned for seventeen months at the hands of the Burmese people.[3]

Besides the physical suffering, the ministry itself was extremely difficult. Judson did not baptize his first convert until six years after he arrived in Burma. Would you put your life on the line and risk your life and the lives of your family members to see only one person come to know Christ? Would you faithfully share the Gospel in the midst of hostility and disease in order to see one convert? Eventually, Judson saw more fruit from his labor, but the ministry was never easy. Judson begged for more missionaries from America to come to Burma and labor alongside of him, but he also warned of the imminent danger. In 1832 he wrote to a group of missionary candidates and sounded this warning:

> Remember, a large proportion of those who come out on a mission to the East die within five years after leaving their native land. Walk softly, therefore; death is narrowly watching your steps.[4]

You might read Judson's account and think he was a crazy man. After all, who in his right mind would put himself and his family in such a dangerous situation? Isn't this kind of life irresponsible? How can a loving husband and father put his wife and children in a position where they are likely to die? Certainly, Judson could have stayed in America, could have served as the pastor of a large church, could have seen more converts in the states than he ever saw in Burma, and he would not have lost his wife and seven of his children to preventable diseases. However, Judson prayed, "your will be done."

Someone even greater than Judson prayed "your will be done." Jesus, on the night before His death, took His disciples to the garden of Gethsemane. At Gethsemane Jesus wrestled with the Father in prayer. His time of prayer was so intense that He poured sweat like drops of blood (Luke 22:44). I cannot begin to imagine that kind of intense praying. I've experienced a range of emotions during times of prayer, but I have never broken out in a sweat. Jesus' prayer was so intense that sweat drops of blood began to pour down His face. What caused such intense, soul-wrenching prayer? Jesus knew the cross was before Him, and the reality of the cross produced an agony in His soul that we will never fully understand. For hours He wrestled in prayer with the Father. In His humanity, Jesus did not want to face the cross. He prayed, "Father, if you are willing, remove this cup from me. Nevertheless, not my will, but yours, be done" (Luke 24:42).

Yes, physical suffering awaited Christ the very next day. He would endure torture at the hands of Roman soldiers; He would endure the agony of being nailed to a cross. He would hang on the cross and literally suffocate to death. The agony of the physical torture of the cross paled in comparison to the agony of drinking from the cup the Father had prepared for Him. The reality is that if humanity had any chance for salvation, someone had to drink from the cup, and Jesus, the only begotten Son of the Father, was the only one who could drink from the cup. This was the will of the Father determined before the foundations of the world. Now the Father's will was coming to fruition. All of eternity waited for this moment in history, and now on the eve of the most important day in history, Jesus experienced the full weight of what lie before Him.

What is the cup Jesus agonized over? In the Old Testament the cup is an expression used to describe the wrath of God. For example, Psalm 75:8 says,

> For in the hand of the Lord there is a cup with foaming wine, well mixed, and he pours out from it, and all the wicked of the earth shall drain it down to the dregs.

Jeremiah 25:15-18 says:

> Thus the Lord, the God of Israel, said to me: 'Take from my hand this cup of the wine of wrath, and make all the

nations to whom I send you drink it. They shall drink and stagger and be crazed because of the sword that I am sending among them.' So I took the cup from the Lord's hand, and made all the nations to whom the Lord sent me drink it: Jerusalem and the cities of Judah, its kings and officials, to make them a desolation and a waste, a hissing and a curse, as at this day...

As horrible as the cross was, the greater horror for Jesus was the awareness that He was going to drink from the cup of God's wrath. On the cross, Jesus carried all the sins of humanity. Isaiah 53:5 says,

But he was pierced for our transgressions; he was crushed for our iniquities; upon him was the chastisement that brought us peace, and with his wounds we are healed.

On the cross, God the Father treated His own Son as if He had committed every murder ever committed. He treated His own Son as if he had uttered every lie ever uttered. He treated His Son as a thief, an adulterer, a slanderer, and every other kind of evil person you can imagine. He treated His own Son as if He had committed every sin ever committed. More than suffering physical pain on the cross, Jesus suffered the full wrath of God.

On that dark day at Calvary, justice was served. The innocent One was punished on behalf of the guilty. Jesus cried out, "My God, my God, why have you forsaken me?" (Mark 15:34) because for the first time in all of eternity, the Son was separated from the Father. The Father, Son, and Holy Spirit had always enjoyed perfect fellowship, but at the moment of Jesus' death, the Father turned away from the Son and poured His wrath out upon Him. Jesus suffered our punishment so we could experience the riches of heaven.

As you reflect on the agony of the cross and the wrath of God being poured out on His Son, you probably better understand why Jesus agonized in prayer in the garden of Gethsemane. Who would want to suffer God's wrath? Who would want to be punished in the place of countless sinners? Yet, in the garden, Jesus prayed in the exact way he had taught his disciples to pray in the Sermon on the Mount. In the midst of His agony Jesus prayed, "Yet not what I will, but what you will."

That prayer cost Jesus His life, and for a moment, it cost Him His eternal relationship with the Father. However, because of what Jesus prayed in the garden, and because of His subsequent obedience, you can be assured that whenever you pray "your will be done, on earth as it is in heaven," it will never cost you your eternal relationship with the Father. Instead, when you pray "your will be done," it will put you in the center of God's will. There is no better place to be than the center of God's will.

When you pray "your will be done," it seems as if you are praying a dangerous prayer because this petition gives God complete control over your life without any objections from you. Doesn't it seem dangerous to let someone else control your life besides you? The truth is we'd like the right to object to God's will when His will doesn't line up with our will. We don't mind God ruling over us as long as it means we don't have to step out of our comfort zones or do anything that seems a bit risky. If God calls us to do something risky, we would really like the option of telling Him, "No!" Praying this petition means we are willing to be completely obedient to God's will, and for many of us, that's asking a bit too much.

What we fail to realize is that being in the center of God's will isn't dangerous at all. You will not find a safer place than the center of God's will. Being in the center of God's doesn't mean that life will be easy for you, or that you won't have to give up anything for the sake of obedience. Being in the center of God's will does mean you can have the full assurance you have lived a life that has brought honor to the God who saved you.

1. How often do you pray for God's will to be done in your life?

2. In what area of your life do you know God's will, but you are refusing to conform to His will?

3. How does reflecting on Jesus' prayer in the garden and His subsequent crucifixion encourage you in your prayer life?

An Informed Petition

You're probably like most Christians when you read this petition. You probably wonder, "What is God's will?" I cannot tell you how many times I have had conversations with people who are trying to "find God's will" for their lives. I've sat across the table with people who in tears have said, "I just want to know God's will for my life!" I understand the anguish in wanting to know God's will. We all want to know God's purpose for our lives. However, is finding God's will that difficult? Is God's will so mysterious that we have to crack some kind of special code to finally discover His purpose?

Discovering God's will is not a guessing game, nor do you need some kind of secret formula or magic password to know His will. He has made His will very obvious in the pages of the Bible. God's will is simply for people to worship Him. That sounds too simple, doesn't it? However, the Bible teaches, and the church has historically taught, that God's will is for us to worship the Lord.

To worship the Lord is to glorify and enjoy the God of all creation. Many churches outside of my denominational background (Southern Baptist) use what are known as catechisms to teach the great doctrines of the faith. A catechism is like a manual designed to give you the basics of the Christian faith. When you hear the word catechism you might think of the Catholic church, but throughout the history of the Protestant church, many Protestant denominations have used catechisms as a discipleship tool. Most catechisms are written in a question/answer style, and perhaps the most famous catechism in the Protestant church is the Westminster Shorter Catechism written in the 1640s. The first question in the Westminster Shorter Catechism is, "What is the chief end of man?" The catechism follows the question with the answer. "Man's chief end is to glorify God, and to enjoy Him forever."

Your purpose, therefore, is to worship the Lord. This is why you were created. This truth is well-illustrated in Joshua 5:13-15. On this long-awaited day Joshua prepared to lead the Hebrew people to overtake Jericho. The Israelites had just crossed into the Promised Land, and they faced the daunting task of driving the Canaanites out of the land. Their first challenge in taking the land of Canaan was to drive the people from the city of Jericho and overtake the city. By this point in Joshua's leadership he was probably feeling extremely confident about himself. God had promised to be with him just as he was with Moses. The people had told Joshua they would follow him. As they prepared to cross the Jordan River God told Joshua He would exalt him before the people. Joshua was the general in charge. He was favored by God and the people. On top of that, the Canaanites already knew about the Hebrew people and their powerful God. They greatly feared the Hebrews and knew their destruction was imminent.

Joshua received a very clear reminder he was not the general in charge that he thought he was. As Joshua approached Jericho he saw a mighty warrior with a sword drawn and ready for battle. Joshua asked, "Whose side are you on?" The warrior responded, "Neither, I am the commander of the Lord's army." I believe that at this moment Joshua was standing before Jesus Christ Himself. This is what theologians call a Christophany or a preincarnate manifestation of Jesus Christ. Joshua immediately realized he was in the presence of the Lord of all creation, and he bowed before Him and asked, "What message do you have for me?" In essence Joshua said, "You tell me what to do." The Mighty Warrior replied by saying, "Take off your shoes. You are standing on holy ground." In this instance God told Joshua the same thing He had told Moses as Moses stood before the burning bush. In essence, the God of all creation said to Joshua, "I want your worship. Worship me."

Don't miss it. God's will for your life is to worship Him. You do not have to lose sleep at night trying to figure out what God wants from you. He wants you to worship Him. How do you worship God? Is worship simply singing songs to God, or is it bowing down and facing a certain direction and reciting certain prayers? Perhaps the Apostle Paul gives us the clearest and most concise definition of worship. Paul writes in Romans 12:1,

> I appeal to you therefore, brothers, by the mercies of God, to present your bodies as a living sacrifice, holy and acceptable to God, which is your spiritual worship.

Worship is presenting your life to Christ and saying, "Whatever you want from me, I am yours. I am laying my life down before you, and you have free reign to do in me and through me whatever you desire." Worship is much more than singing songs or attending religious services. Worship is a life of surrendered obedience presented to the Father in response to what He has done for us through Jesus Christ.

If God's will is for you to worship Him, what does that mean about the specifics of your life? Is it God's will for you to move to a remote village in Africa and spend your life making disciples among people who have never heard of Jesus? Is it God's will for you to lead a small group or teach a Sunday School class? Is it God's will for you to go to college and become a nurse? God's will is for you to worship Him, and wherever you find yourself, whether it is in a remote village in Africa or working the night shift at a local factory, you can accomplish God's will. Whether you end up on the mission field in one of the most difficult places in the world or in the NICU unit of a local hospital largely depends on how God has specifically created you and spiritually gifted you.

If you are surrendered to Him, and if you are praying, "your will be done on earth as it is in heaven," you can rest assured that God will place you exactly where He desires you to be in order to accomplish exactly what He desires to accomplish in you and through you.

Here's the question. Are you willing to worship God by submitting your life to Him in full surrender? Are you willing to say, "As an act of devotion and worship, I'm willing to go wherever you might send me and do whatever you tell me"? Are you willing to go to the furthest parts of the world if He calls you? Or, if God chooses to keep you in your hometown all the days of your life, are you willing to stay in your hometown and faithfully serve Him by making disciples locally, supporting global disciple-making, and living in obedience to His Word? Are you willing to worship God by saying, "Whatever it is you want from me, I'm willing to do"? If that is your attitude towards God, you are not going to spend a lot of time guessing what you ought to do because you will simply use every opportunity God presents to obey what He has already told you to do in His Word, and as you use every opportunity He gives you to worship Him through your obedience, He will make it abundantly clear to you how He wants you to serve Him.

Notice again what Jesus says. He teaches us to pray "your will be done on earth." The ultimate goal is not simply your individual worship of God. The ultimate goal is that every person on the face of the planet will gladly worship our Lord. Carefully read Psalm 96 and think about your responsibility to declare God's glory among the nations so all people will know our God is worthy of the worship of every person on the face of the planet.

> Oh sing to the Lord a new song; sing to the Lord, all the earth! Sing to the Lord, bless his name; tell of his salvation from day to day. Declare his glory among the nations, his marvelous works among all the peoples! For great is the Lord, and greatly to be praised; he is to be feared above all gods. For all the gods of the peoples are worthless idols, but the Lord made the heavens. Splendor and majesty are before him; strength and beauty are in his sanctuary. Ascribe to the Lord, O families of the peoples, ascribe to the Lord glory and strength! Ascribe to the Lord the glory due his name; bring an offering, and come into his courts! Worship the Lord in the splendor of holiness; tremble before him, all the earth! Say among the nations, "The Lord

reigns! Yes, the world is established; it shall never be moved; he will judge the peoples with equity." Let the heavens be glad, and let the earth rejoice; let the sea roar, and all that fills it; let the field exult, and everything in it! Then shall all the trees of the forest sing for joy before the Lord, for he comes, for he comes to judge the earth. He will judge the world in righteousness, and the peoples in his faithfulness.

What hinders God's will from being accomplished? Ultimately, sin hinders God's will from being accomplished. At times, even as a believer, you'd rather not worship the Lord. You'd rather give your allegiance to something or someone else. You and I have a tendency to make work, family, sports, or money supreme in our lives rather than make Jesus supreme in our lives. You and I would rather ignore God's call to declare His glory because at times we fail to worship Him as our glorious God. To pray "your will be done," is to ask God to help you again to see how glorious He is so you might be compelled to worship Him and make His glory known to those who do not yet know Him.

The reality is that in this age not all will worship Christ. However, a day will come when all will acknowledge Jesus Christ as Lord and bow their knee to Him. Scripture makes this promise clear in Philippians 2:9-11.

> Therefore God has highly exalted him and bestowed on him the name that is above every name, so that at the name of Jesus every knee should bow, in heaven and on earth and under the earth, and every tongue confess that Jesus Christ is Lord, to the glory of God the Father.

Everyone will bow in submission to the Lord, but not everyone will bow in gratitude. Many will bow in shame as they recognize how they wasted their lives on this earth by living for their own glory rather than the glory of God. However, those of us who have consistently prayed, "your will be done" will bow in gratitude to the God who has saved us and used us to make His glory known to the ends of the earth.

4. *Before reading this chapter how would you have defined God's will? How would you have defined worship?*

5. *Why do you think we are tempted to look for God's will in places other than His Word?*

6. *What hinders you from worshipping God in the way Paul describes in Romans 12:1?*

7. *How should Romans 12:1 affect the ministry of the local church?*

A Delightful Petition

Jesus teaches us to pray, "Your will be done on earth as it is in heaven." In heaven God's will is done perfectly and joyfully. Who in heaven ever objects to what God desires? Who in heaven ever questions God? No one in heaven objects to God's will because in heaven sin does not hinder anyone from doing what God has called them to do. In heaven there is no pride, selfish ambition, apathy, or any other form of disobedience. What God says is done immediately. In heaven one does not ask how obedience to God's will might affect the way others think about him or how obedience might interfere with his own agenda. In heaven no one gives God excuses as to why he did not obey. God's will is done perfectly.

Obviously, we do not live in heaven yet. We live in a world that is stained with sin. We will never obey God perfectly on this earth, but we long for perfect obedience. Jesus told His followers in the Sermon on the Mount, "You therefore must be perfect, as your heavenly Father is perfect" (Matthew 5:48). Jesus obviously knew we would never be perfect this side of eternity, but someday, when Christ has finished His sanctifying work within us and has given us a glorified body, we will obey perfectly.

While we will never be perfect this side of eternity, the more we walk in intimacy with the Lord, the more we will conform to the will of God. Walking in intimacy with the Lord is the key to doing His will. On earth, as we submit to the work of the Holy Spirit, He will bring us into deeper intimacy with the Father, and the more intimately we know the

Father, the less obedience will be an issue for us. The more we walk with the Lord the more we realize obedience to His will is our natural response to the salvation He has given us.

In heaven living out God's will is a delight and an absolute joy. No one complains about doing His will. No one walks around heaven saying, "I wish we could do something else besides serve the Lord." Consider the picture of God's throne room that John paints in the Book of Revelation.

> ...and before the throne there was as it were a sea of glass, like crystal. And around the throne, on each side of the throne, are four living creatures, full of eyes in front and behind: the first living creature like a lion, the second living creature like an ox, the third living creature with the face of a man, and the fourth living creature like an eagle in flight. And the four living creatures, each of them with six wings, are full of eyes all around and within, and day and night they never cease to say, "Holy, holy, holy, is the Lord God Almighty, who was and is and is to come!" And whenever the living creatures give glory and honor and thanks to him who is seated on the throne, who lives forever and ever, the twenty-four elders fall down before him who is seated on the throne and worship him who lives forever and ever. They cast their crowns before the throne, saying, "Worthy are you, our Lord and God, to receive glory and honor and power, for you created all things, and by your will they existed and were created." (Revelation 4:6-11)

You get the idea that these elders are pretty important people. We don't know exactly who these elders are. Some think they are angelic beings while others believe they are redeemed people who God has crowned for their faithfulness to Him. Personally, I believe these are redeemed people of God who have been crowned for their faithfulness. Can you imagine what it must be like for the King of kings to place a crown on your head as a reward for faithfulness? Notice what the elders do with their crowns. In no way do they hold on to their crowns and bask in their own glory. Instead, they toss their crowns to the ground as they recognize they are not worthy to be crowned. These elders know that only Jesus is worthy to be crowned. As they toss their crowns before His throne they cry out in worship. This scene in Revelation is absolutely breathtaking, and every single one of us will respond to the Lord in the same way that the elders respond to Him. I don't think for a moment that as the elders cast their crowns before the Lord's throne one of them turns to the other and says, "You know, I really like my crown. It's so beautiful and shiny. I think I'm going to keep it for myself. You go ahead and toss yours, but I'm going to hold on to mine." In heaven God is worshipped perfectly, and these elders gladly lay everything down before God's throne as an act of worship.

Why do these elders gladly worship? In God's presence they understand fully what God has done for them. God has rescued them from their sin. They, like us, were hell-bound because of their disobedience to the Father. But, God entered into our world as a man to rescue us from the grip of hell. The One who is eternally infinite stepped into a finite world of sin and rebellion and subjected Himself to this cruel world. Jesus did what we could not do. He lived a perfect life on our behalf and went to the cross taking what we deserve so that we can get what we do not deserve. These elders that surround the throne of God understand what we so easily forget. We easily forget the sacrifice made for us that has brought us into a relationship with the Father. We easily forget that because of His sacrifice, our God is worthy of our praise and adoration. He is worthy of us gladly and without question submitting to His will.

What about you? Do you gladly submit to God's will? Psalm 100:2 says, "Serve the Lord with gladness." If you aren't so glad when you serve the Lord, you are not in the Lord's will. God's will is that you worship Him with gladness. Worshiping the Lord is a delight because we know the price that has been paid to free us from our sin, and we know the absolute intimacy we have with Him. You will never be joyless living in the center of God's will, even if living in God's will means it puts you in difficult or tragic circumstances. When you begin to understand the depths of God's love for you demonstrated on the cross, you will always be able to worship and serve Him with gladness even when life is tough.

Pray for God's will to be done in your life. Place your life before Him, as Paul describes in Romans 12:1, and tell God, "Here I am, all of me, for your pleasure." You will never regret placing your life in the hands of God. You will never regret living in the center of His will. You will never regret living for His glory and making Him known in this world. On the other hand, you will regret not living in the center of His will. You will regret not giving Him free reign over your life. You will regret disobedience. If you will never regret living in God's will, and you will often regret living out of God's will, praying for God's will to be done on earth as it is in heaven is essential to your prayer life.

The constant question you should ask God is, "Lord, am I cooperating with the work of your Spirit and allowing Him to conform me to your will? If not, please discipline me so I will be submissive to your Spirit's work." Will you be bold enough to constantly pray, "your will be done on earth as it is in heaven"?

8. Do you delight in God's will for your life? Why or why not?

9. How does thinking about how God's will is carried out in heaven motivate you to carry out God's will on earth?

[6]

Give Us Our Daily Bread

PUTTING YOUR NEEDS IN PERSPECTIVE

WE FINALLY GET TO a petition in the Disciple's Prayer that teaches us to focus on the things we need. Mastering this petition shouldn't be a problem at all. You probably already have a long list of things you are asking God to do for you. The way this petition starts excites our selfish imaginations. "Give us…" That sounds good, doesn't it? Didn't you come to Christ, in part, because of what you get as a Christian? Maybe when you gave your life to Jesus it was because someone shared the Gospel with you and told you that if you did not turn from your sins and trust Christ as Lord, you would go to hell. You were told if you prayed a simple prayer you would get heaven instead of hell. Perhaps someone told you about the streets of gold and how there would be no tears and no sickness in heaven. You were told you would live forever. That sounded good to you, so you prayed the sinner's prayer because you didn't want hell, and who doesn't want an eternal life free from suffering?

Hopefully, you have matured enough in your relationship with Christ to understand the Christian faith is not about *what* you get but *who* you get. Sure, heaven will be great. No tears, disease, or death will be wonderful, but would heaven be heaven without Jesus? Certainly, God gives us good gifts. Eternity is a wonderful gift of God that we will inherit. God also gives us many good gifts to enjoy on this side of eternity. He gives us the gift of family, the gift of friendship, the gift of marriage, the gift of material possessions, and countless other gifts. A week of vacation at the beach is a good gift from God. A nice home to enjoy as a retreat from the rest of the world is a good gift from God. God gives His children good gifts, and we are not wrong for enjoying the gifts of God whether they are eternal or temporal. However, when you and I enjoy the gifts more than the giver of the gifts, we have missed the point.

The reality is that the gifts will never ultimately satisfy you. Your spouse is a good gift from God, but your spouse cannot ultimately satisfy you. Your children cannot ultimately satisfy, nor can your nice house in the suburbs. Even the gift of a loving church family cannot ultimately satisfy you. God has given you countless gifts to enjoy, but they do not ultimately satisfy. Rather, the gifts point to the One who ultimately satisfies. Jesus alone ultimately satisfies. If only Jesus ultimately satisfies, then your primary pursuit in life should be Him and not the gifts He chooses to give you.

You will experience seasons in life in which blessings from the hand of God seem scarce. Maybe you've already experienced seasons of great physical need in your life. In those seasons, was Jesus enough for you? If Jesus is the object of your worship and affection, then He will always be enough for you, even when you have little. Paul understood this well. In Philippians 4:11-13 Paul writes,

> ...for I have learned in whatever situation I am to be content. I know how to be brought low, and I know how to abound. In any and every circumstance, I have learned the secret of facing plenty and hunger, abundance and need. I can do all things through him who strengthens me.

All Paul really needed was Jesus, and his faith in Christ sustained him through all of life's circumstances. Paul's focus was on Jesus and not merely the gifts Jesus gave. Jesus does teach us in the Disciple's Prayer to pray for the things we need, but we should pray for the things we need with the understanding that ultimately Jesus is the bread of life. In John 6:35 Jesus said, "I am the bread of life; whoever comes to me shall not hunger, and whoever believes in me shall never thirst." Do not forget that ultimately Jesus is the bread you need to feast on daily.

I think the reason Jesus teaches us to pray "give us this day our daily bread" in the middle of the Disciple's Prayer is to help us put our needs in perspective. If you use the Disciple's Prayer as a model for your own prayer life, then before you pray through this petition you've already prayed about what you need most. What you need most is not for your physical needs to be met. Rather, what you need most is an intimate relationship with God the Father that results in worship, and you need to be obedient to His will. Concern yourself with your relationship with God and being obedient to His will, and He will take care of your daily needs.

This petition is in the middle of the Disciple's Prayer to remind you once again that you are not ultimate; God is. Yes, God will provide for you, and yes, you should ask for His provisions, but His worship and the advancement of His kingdom are a much higher priority than your needs being met. If you are seeking to know God instead of simply asking God to take care of all your needs, it will radically change the way you ask things of God. Instead of asking God for what you want, you simply will ask God to give you exactly what you need to accomplish His will. Pray this petition because you understand you are absolutely dependent on God to give you everything you need to accomplish His will. Praying because you depend on God for everything, even your daily bread, destroys some sinful tendencies, which we'll examine, that lurk deep within the recesses of your heart.

1. *Does your prayer life focus on what you need or on who you need?*

2. *How can you learn to be content like the Apostle Paul?*

3. How can you enjoy God's gifts without making the gifts of God more important to you than God Himself?

Depending on God for Everything Destroys Self-Sufficiency

To ask the God of all creation for bread seems so menial. You can get bread without God's help, can't you? If you are a prisoner, bread is a part of your room and board. If you are homeless, you can go to a local soup kitchen and easily get bread. Getting bread doesn't require you to be a law-abiding citizen nor does it require you to have a job. Bread is plentiful and readily available. If bread is plentiful, why should you ask for bread? Certainly, in some impoverished countries of Africa or Asia it makes sense to pray for bread, but not in the United States of America. You and I do not need God's help to get bread, but we do need help with the bigger issues of life. We need help raising our children, climbing the corporate ladder, and staying physically well. Shouldn't we skip praying for bread and jump right into asking God for the things we really need?

You could skip over praying for bread and begin asking God for the big things, but you do need bread. You do need food to survive, and this petition teaches us that ultimately God is our provider. You have food on the table not because you live in a country that has an abundance of bread, nor because you have a job that provides you with a salary so you can buy bread. You have bread on the table because in His mercy and grace God chooses to provide you with bread. As much as you think you are, ultimately you are not your own provider, and you are not the ultimate provider of your family. God is your provider, and whether you acknowledge it or not, you are dependent on Him for everything, even the bread you bought at Kroger.

Self-sufficiency plagues our lives. We love our independence. We love to boast about what we can accomplish through hard work and ingenuity. We certainly do not want to be thought of as needy people who have to depend on God for something as simple as bread. Sure, we need God to help us with the catastrophes of life that we cannot seem to handle on our own. We want God's help to get out of a financial mess or deal with rebellious teenagers. However, we can handle most things without him. At least that's what we think, and that kind of thinking is extremely dangerous because it leads us to trust ourselves more than we trust God. We cannot do anything without the help of God. We are dependent on God for every breath we take. We are dependent on God for good health to be able to work so we can buy bread. We are dependent on God to provide us with family and friends to love us and help us. We are dependent on God to provide us with everything we need, even the most insignificant, minute details of life. Do not lose sight of the reality that God is in control of everything.

To pray "give us our daily bread" is to humble yourself before God. When you ask God to provide for your most basic needs you are admitting you are not self-sufficient but extremely needy. Jesus said in Matthew 5:3, "Blessed are the poor in spirit, for theirs is the kingdom of heaven."

Several years ago, I took a team from my church on a short-term mission trip to Russia and saw firsthand how the poor in spirit are blessed. For several days we ministered in a small village of several hundred people in which no Protestant church exists. We spent several days encouraging the few believers who lived in that village. We spent time with about a dozen believing ladies and one believing man. This handful of believers, most of whom were elderly, had no organized church and were in desperate need of encouragement. In this particular village these believers were thought to be a part of a cult and were ostracized and persecuted in their community, but they clung to Jesus knowing that He was all they had and all they needed.

After a day or so of spending time with these believers, the missionary and his wife took my wife and me to the home of an elderly lady to share the Lord's Supper with her. This lady was the matriarch of the small Christian community. Stricken to her home because of her rapidly failing health, this lady must have been close to ninety-years-old. By all accounts, her life seemed miserable. She lived in an old, run-down home. She had no family to take care of her, and she spent most of her life ostracized from her community because of her faith. In spite of her circumstances she was the most joyous woman I have ever met. She knew the end of her life was near, and she knew better days were ahead of her. She cried out for the grace of God that night as she longed to depart from this earth and finally be with her Lord for whom she had sacrificed so much. In tears she explained how precious Jesus was to her and how desperately she needed her Savior. She talked about her desire for her rundown home to be a meeting house for believers after her death. She talked about her desire to see the young people in her village reached for Christ as she reflected on her community's desperate need for the Gospel.

This frail, dying woman was the epitome of someone who's poor in spirit. At the end of her life all she had was Jesus, and all she needed was Jesus. I have no doubt in my mind that the kingdom of heaven belongs to her just as Jesus promised in Matthew 5:3. I have never experienced the Lord's Supper as powerfully as I did that night knowing this elderly woman who consumed the Lord's body and blood in the symbols of bread and wine would soon be in the presence of the risen Lord. Soon she would touch the literal body of Christ that was broken for her. In that small room we celebrated how the life and death of Jesus had completely changed this woman even though it had cost her everything. That night I longed to be as poor and needy as she was so I too might fully desire the riches of the eternal kingdom of God that awaits me.

Jesus tells us it is only those who see their neediness and cry out in desperation for the grace of God who will inherit the kingdom of heaven. You might think you are self-sufficient, but you are not. You might think you don't need anyone or anything, but you are wrong. You are not able to take care of yourself. You are just as needy as the most poverty-stricken person you know, and you are utterly dependent on God. Admit it and cry out to Him. Ask God to satisfy you by giving you the spiritual bread found in Jesus Christ and ask Him to teach you to depend on Him for your daily needs. Learn to thank Him for any ability He has given you that enables you to provide for yourself and your family. Everything, even the smallest blessings of life, is from the hand of God.

When we learn to trust God with the small things we will have no problem trusting Him with the big things. Because of our self-sufficiency, many of us have not learned how to depend on God in the small things. Therefore, when tragedies occur we run to God in desperation, hoping He will help us, rather than running to Him in full confidence knowing He is our help in time of need. When difficulties arise we run to God as our last resort because we have run out of other options. When we learn to trust God in the small things, we will have no problem trusting Him when difficult days arise. We will know He is our help because we have seen Him at work in the minute details of our everyday lives.

4. When was the last time you thanked God for providing you with your daily needs?

5. How has your own self-sufficiency kept you from trusting God?

Depending on God for Everything Destroys Worry

Knowing God cares about our daily, physical needs should remind us of the magnitude of His love for us. God is a good Father who not only showers us with more than we need, but He also gives us exactly what we need each day. If this is true, we have no reason to worry about our daily needs. Why worry about where we are going to find the resources to survive when we know God gives us exactly what we need? God might not give us exactly what we want, but we do not have to worry about our daily provisions.

You remember the story of the Hebrew people wandering in the wilderness for forty years. If they weren't so hard headed they would have spent much less time in the wilderness. Like us, they were slow learners and stubborn. In spite of their stubbornness and disobedience God took care of them. Every morning when they got up manna, a bread-like substance, covered the ground. All the Hebrews had to do was gather what they needed for the day. They didn't have to spend their days hunting and gathering. Manna wasn't necessarily what the Hebrews wanted every day, but it is what God determined they needed. Instead of spending their days hunting for their own food, they spent their days following God's presence as He led them through the wilderness. Their focus was to be on God rather than focusing on satisfying their needs. When they tried to hoard manna for the following day it would spoil overnight. God provided their daily bread, and the Hebrews had to learn to trust that each day God would be faithful to give exactly what they needed.

Maybe you are a parent with a small child. Does your child worry about where his next meal is coming from? Absolutely not, because your child knows you are going to provide for him. Your child is free to enjoy a relationship with you without worrying about the necessities of life because your child is confident in your ability to provide. Likewise, Jesus teaches us we do not have to worry about the necessities of life. Rather than worrying, we are free to focus on seeking His kingdom and growing in intimacy with Him. He will take care of us, and when our focus is on growing in Christ, He will teach us to be content with whatever He gives us. Right after teaching the disciples how to pray, Jesus challenged his disciples not to worry. Consider Matthew 6:25-34:

> Therefore I tell you, do not be anxious about your life, what you will eat or what you will drink, nor about your body, what you will put on. Is not life more than food, and the body more than clothing? Look at the birds of the air: they neither sow nor reap nor gather into barns, and yet your heavenly Father feeds them. Are you not of more value than they? And which of you by being anxious can add a single hour to his span of life? And why are you anxious about clothing? Consider the lilies of the field, how they grow: they neither toil nor spin, yet I tell you, even Solomon in all his glory was not arrayed like one of these. But if God so clothes the grass of the field, which today is alive and tomorrow is thrown into the oven, will he not much more clothe you, O you of little faith? Therefore do not be anxious, saying, "What shall we eat?" or "What shall we drink?" or "What shall we wear?" For the Gentiles seek after all these things, and your heavenly Father knows that you need them all. But seek first the kingdom of God and his righteousness, and all these things

will be added to you. Therefore do not be anxious about tomorrow, for tomorrow will be anxious for itself. Sufficient for the day is its own trouble.

The point of this passage is clear. If God provides for things that are of infinitely less value than you and me, then why wouldn't He provide for us? Obviously, Jesus does not promote laziness. We cannot go around thinking, "Since God is my provider I don't have to worry about getting a job. I can relax, and He'll send the pizza delivery boy to my house every day." Jesus challenges us to look at the birds. Birds are not lazy. They are extremely industrious. You know the old saying, "The early bird catches the worm." Birds work for their food, but they do not worry about their food. Hard work honors the Lord. God is always at work, and when we work we imitate His character. However, as we work, we don't have to worry.

This might come as a shock to you if you struggle with worry, but worry is a sin. Since Jesus tells us in this passage of Scripture not to worry, you are disobeying the Lord's command whenever you worry. Think about why worry is sinful. When you worry you demonstrate a lack of trust in the promises of God. Consider what Tim Keller says about worry and anxiety.

> Anxiety is this. Anxiety is essentially saying, "Father, you emptied heaven of your greatest treasure and you executed your Son voluntarily for me and I'm not sure you're going to know how to arrange my week."[1]

Worry is always a lack of trust in your heavenly Father. If you ever doubt that God is able to take care of even the most menial needs of life, go to the cross and see what He has already done for you. If He has already emptied heaven for you, surely he can take care of all of your other needs. Worry not only demonstrates a lack of trust, it is also an insult to your heavenly Father. How would you like it if your child walked around the house doubting your ability to take care of him? What if your child said, "Dad, you are not competent enough to take care of me"? Isn't that essentially what we are saying to God when we choose not to trust Him? Besides, as Jesus points out, worry is not going to add a single day to your life. In fact, the opposite might be true. All kinds of chronic medical conditions are often the result of worry and stress.

You deal with worry by confessing it as sin and repenting of it. You are probably familiar with the term repentance, but do you know how to repent? Repentance is turning from a sinful behavior and exchanging it for Christ-exalting behavior. Don't forget that as a believer you are a new person in Christ. As a new person in Christ you are daily exchanging sinful habits that are a result of your old, sinful self for habits that characterize who you are in Christ. Paul wrote in Ephesians 4:20-24,

> But that is not the way you learned Christ! — assuming that you have heard about him and were taught in him, as the truth is in Jesus, to put off your old self, which belongs to your former manner of life and is corrupt through deceitful desires, and to be renewed in the spirit of your minds, and to put on the new self, created after the likeness of God in true righteousness and holiness.

Paul gives several examples of how to put off the old self and put on the new in the verses that follow. If you have a problem with lying, Paul challenges you to start telling the truth. If you have a problem with stealing, Paul challenges you to get a job. Exchange the sinful behavior for a Christ-exalting behavior. Obviously, exchanging any sinful behavior for a Christ-honoring behavior requires the help of the Holy Spirit. You cannot crucify sin and put on the new self without Him. Ask for His help.

In Matthew 6:33 Jesus gives the Christ-honoring behavior that you should exchange for worry. Instead of being a worrier, become a kingdom seeker. We already discussed the kingdom of God in a previous chapter, and we discovered that a kingdom seeker is one who is concerned over and above everything else about the reign and rule of God in this world. If you are concerned with God's kingdom more than anything else, His kingdom will consume you, and you simply will not have the time to be consumed by worry. What consumes you: worry or the kingdom of God?

In light of what Paul teaches, "give us our daily bread" could be a prayer of repentance for you. You could pray this petition in this way,

> *Father, I recognize that I am preoccupied with my own needs. My worry over material possessions hinders me from seeking your kingdom. Forgive me and teach me to trust that you will take care of my every need. You are my Father who loves me, and I have no need to doubt you.*

Do not let worry rob you of the joy of being consumed with the Father's love and a heart for His kingdom.

This petition is teaching us to walk by faith in every area of our lives. It's simple to enter the kingdom by faith, but it's quite difficult to live by faith. To enter the kingdom of God you simply have to believe in the Gospel, but to walk by faith you have to live by the Gospel. In those moments you are tempted to worry or tempted to trust in your own self-sufficiency, go back to the cross. Remember how your Father demonstrated His love for you by crushing His only begotten Son so you could be brought into a right relationship with Him. If you will remember the Gospel, you will live by the Gospel as you daily trust His grace and His sufficiency for you.

6. *What hinders you from trusting God fully?*

7. *What do you most often worry about? Why do you worry about that? How do you think seeking the kingdom of God first will alleviate your worry?*

8. *If God already knows how He is going to provide for you, why does He want you to pray for daily bread?*

Depending on God for Everything Destroys Selfishness

I've never been in real need. The only time I have come close to being in real need was after Hurricane Katrina. During Katrina I lived in Franklinton, Louisiana, just sixty miles north of New Orleans, where I pastored a small, country church. Thankfully, I did not suffer near the loss of those who actually lived in New Orleans, but the eye of the storm came right through Franklinton. The town lost about seventy percent of its timber. The damage caused by Katrina was an unbelievable sight. Downed trees and power lines caused much damage in our community. It looked like a bomb had been detonated in our community. It seemed like every home had been wrecked by falling trees. When I returned from evacuating, I found a tree in my living room when I walked through the front door of my home.

While the damage was significant, what was more torturous at the time was facing a hot and humid Louisiana August with no electricity. For five long weeks we had no electricity, and since Franklinton is a very rural area, most of us had no running water because we depended on well-water drawn from the ground with electric pumps. To say that those five weeks were miserable is an understatement.

A week or so after the storm, relief organizations such as the Red Cross and FEMA set up operations in Franklinton. My daily routine included going to the gas station at 6:00 in the morning to wait for two hours in line to purchase overpriced gas to run my generator. Then I would head to the local park to receive a bag of ice, bottled water, and government-issued MRE's. (I feel for our soldiers who have to eat those MRE's on a regular basis.) Some days, the Red Cross would serve a hot meal, and I would get in line to receive a hot meal. Times were tough.

As thankful as I am for FEMA and the Red Cross' response to Hurricane Katrina, I was even more thankful for the response of the church in which I grew up. My home church knew of the challenges we faced in Franklinton. They prayed fervently for me and the congregation I served. Not only did they pray for me and my congregation, they also became the answer to our prayers. We were asking God for daily bread. We were asking God to meet our physical needs, and as we prayed, my home church collected a tractor-trailer full of non-perishable foods, bottled water, batteries, generators, and other items that were so critical during that time. My home church also sent teams of people to assist our church in ministering to our community by helping us remove trees from homes and debris from yards. While Hurricane Katrina was not an experience I want to repeat, through that tragic event I saw the church rise up to be the hands and feet of Jesus during a great time of need. God used my home church to give us needy people in Franklinton daily bread.

Do not miss the plural pronoun in this petition. "Give *us* this day *our* daily bread." With this petition Jesus teaches us that we're not only to pray for our individual needs, we are also to pray for the needs of others. We see examples of people praying for others often in Scripture. For example, look at the letters Paul wrote to different churches in the New Testament. Repeatedly, he reminds believers he is praying for them. In Philippians 1:3, Paul writes to the believers in Philippi, "I thank my God in all my remembrance of you, always in every prayer of mine for you all making my prayer with joy, because of your partnership in the gospel from the first day until now." In Ephesians 1:16, Paul writes to the believers in Ephesus, "I do not cease to give thanks for you, remembering you in my prayers…" In James 5:14, James reminds church leaders to pray over those who are sick. He writes, "Is anyone among you sick? Let him call for the elders of the church, and let them pray over him, anointing him with oil in the name of the Lord."

You are to pray for those who are hurting, those who are sick, and those who are without. As you pray for others, be sensitive to the Spirit of God because often times as you pray for the needs of others God will show you how He wants you to minister to the very people for whom you are praying. Be a praying person, but also be a person of action. Show the love of Christ not just in praying for others, but also in practically demonstrating the love of Christ to those who are hurting and in need. This petition destroys selfishness because when you are praying for the needs of others, God will take your focus off of you and place it on others. God will show you ways you can minister to the hurting. As you pray for your needs and the needs of others, ask God how you might be an encouragement and a source of strength and provision for the people for whom you are praying. Watch God destroy your selfish ways as you pray for the daily bread of others.

This petition is not a selfish petition at all, and you probably are not as good at praying for your needs as you might think. Praying for your daily needs means you come to God as a poor and needy beggar on behalf of yourself confessing your dependency on Him.

Come to God with empty hands and know you have nothing except what He gives you. Know as you come to God with empty hands, He will fill those hands with exactly what you need.

9. In what ways have you seen God provide your daily bread through other people?

10. How has God used you to provide the daily bread of someone who is hurting? Have you been asking God to show you how to minister to others who are hurting?

11. How can the church do a better job of praying for daily bread?

[7]

Forgiveness

Receiving Forgiveness

YOU MIGHT EXPECT JESUS to teach us to seek God's forgiveness earlier rather than later in the Disciple's Prayer, but Jesus is very purposeful in how He teaches us to pray. He places seeking forgiveness later in the Disciple's Prayer because confession flows out of adoration and worship. As we hallow God's name, seek His kingdom and perfect will, and throw ourselves on Him in complete dependency, we are humbled. We see God for who He is, and we see how sinful we are. A right view of God will always give us a right view of our own sin. The more we see God high and exalted, the more we will recognize the horror of our own sin, and the more we will cry out to God in confession and repentance.

This was the case with Isaiah. After the death of King Uzziah, during a time of national mourning, Isaiah entered the temple and saw God sitting on a throne. Isaiah 6:1-3 records Isaiah's vision:

> In the year that King Uzziah died I saw the Lord sitting upon a throne, high and lifted up; and the train of his robe filled the temple. Above him stood the seraphim. Each had six wings: with two he covered his face, and with two he covered his feet, and with two he flew. And one called to another and said: "Holy, holy, holy is the Lord of hosts; the whole earth is full of his glory!"

Isaiah was overwhelmed when he saw the exalted Lord, and his response was the natural response we all have when we see God for who He is: confession. Isaiah said in response to his vision of the exalted Lord,

> Woe is me! For I am lost; for I am a man of unclean lips, and I dwell in the midst of a people of unclean lips; for my eyes have seen the King, the Lord of hosts. (Isaiah 6:5)

When we see God for who He is, our natural response will be to confess our sins and seek His forgiveness. This is why Jesus teaches us to acknowledge God's holiness before we confess our own sin.

You and I do not understand how terrible our sin is before our holy God. God absolutely hates sin because it is an attack on His perfect nature. Sin is absolute rebellion against the God who created us for His purposes. Whenever you sin you essentially are waving your fist in the air toward God and saying to Him, "You do not know what is best for my life, and you are not my boss. I am in control of my life, and I do not need you." If you are a parent you would be hurt and angered if your child spoke to you that way. In a much greater sense, God is infinitely angry with sinners who treat Him with such disdain.

The Bible doesn't pull any punches in regard to the horror of sin and God's hatred of it. Consider Psalm 5:4-6.

> For you are not a God who delights in wickedness; evil may not dwell with you. The boastful shall not stand before your eyes; you hate all evildoers. You destroy those who speak lies; the Lord abhors the bloodthirsty and deceitful man.

Psalm 11:5-7 is just as stern.

> The Lord tests the righteous, but his soul hates the wicked and the one who loves violence. Let him rain coals on the wicked; fire and sulfur and a scorching wind shall be the portion of their cup. For the Lord is righteous; he loves righteous deeds; the upright shall behold his face.

God destroys sinners. His wrath burns against all who rebel against Him. The bad news is we are sinners, and we cannot do anything about it. Sin is a part of our nature. We can't help but sin apart from the Spirit's work within us. We are born rebellious against God, and we deserve to be destroyed. The good news is God has chosen to extend His love to those against whom His wrath burns. In Romans 5:6-8, Paul writes,

> For while we were still weak, at the right time Christ died for the ungodly. For one will scarcely die for a righteous person—though perhaps for a good person one would dare even to die—but God shows his love for us in that while we were still sinners, Christ died for us.

You deserved to be destroyed. God's wrath burned against you, but at the same time, He chose to love you in spite of your sin. God didn't choose to love you because of anything you did but simply because He is gracious and merciful. In His grace and mercy, He gave His Son who died in your place. The Father punished His perfect Son so you could be forgiven of your rebellion against the God who created you, and so you could have a new life indwelt and empowered by His Holy Spirit.

If you have surrendered your life to Jesus Christ, you are completely forgiven of your sins. Instead of God destroying you, He is making you new, and He does not hold one sin that you have ever committed or ever will commit against you. Jesus fully paid the penalty of your sin. He took your punishment for you. David writes in Psalm 103:11-12,

> For as high as the heavens are above the earth, so great is his steadfast love toward those who fear him; as far as the east is from the west, so far does he remove our transgressions from us.

In the Book of Hebrews, God says to His people,

> For I will be merciful toward their iniquities, and I will remember their sins no more. (Hebrews 8:12)

God has completely removed your sin, and He doesn't even remember your sin. To be sure, God doesn't forget anything. He is all knowing. God does remember exactly how you rebelled against Him. He remembers that you were once an object of His wrath. However, because of the work of Christ on the cross God treats you as if He doesn't remember your sin. He treats you as if it never happened. When you stand before the God of all creation on Judgment Day you will not be judged for your rebellion against God because in Christ your sin has been cast as far as the east is from the west.

If this gracious act of God's love does not inspire you to surrender daily to Him as an act of worship, then you probably have never experienced His grace.

1. In light of Psalm 5:4-6 and 11:5-7, how should you respond to the common saying, "God hates sin but loves the sinner"?

2. How should the reality that God remembers your sin no more help you overcome guilt for your past sins?

Seeking Forgiveness

If God has completely forgiven you of your sins, and if He remembers them no more, then why would Jesus teach us in the Disciple's Prayer to pray, "Forgive us our debts as we also have forgiven our debtors"? Why ask for forgiveness of sins if you have already been forgiven? You ask because you are still a sinner, and sin affects your daily walk with the Lord. Even though you are God's child, and even though He is changing you and conforming you to Jesus, you are still battling with your old sinful nature. Remnants of your old sin nature are still present, and you will battle with your old nature until Christ calls you home to be with Him. While all of your past, present, and future sins have been forgiven, you are a work in progress who will still sins even after you come to Christ. Therefore, continual confession and repentance are necessary.

When you trusted Christ as Lord and Savior, you entered into a covenant relationship with the God of all creation. You are His child and that will never change. Being His child does not change the fact that you sin. Thankfully, the Holy Spirit will convict you when you sin, and you will grow in your desire to obey the Lord. However, you will always struggle with sin. The Apostle Paul was very transparent about his own struggle with sin. Paul wrote in Romans 7:18-20:

> For I know that nothing good dwells in me, that is, in my flesh. For I have the desire to do what is right, but not the ability to carry it out. For I do not do the good I want, but the evil I do not want is what I keep on doing. Now if I do what I do not want, it is no longer I who do it, but sin that dwells within me.

As a believer you probably feel much like Paul. You want to do good, and you see progress in your walk with the Lord. You see seasons of obedience, but it seems like as soon as you take a step forward in your walk with the Lord, you take two steps back. You will always have this struggle. While you will grow in obedience to the Lord as you grow in your relationship with Him, you will never be completely free from sin in this life. Thankfully, as a believer, your sin will never separate you from the love of God. Because of His covenant love for you and because of your faith in Christ, God's wrath no longer burns against you. His wrath toward your sin was satisfied at the cross.

Your sin will not change your position before God if you are in Christ, but your sin will affect your fellowship with God. It's much like a marital relationship. Staci is my wife, and only death can change our marital union. She married me for better or for worse, and worse seems to creep up quite a bit in a marital relationship. I sin against my wife often, but because we entered into a covenant relationship, my sin does not change the fact that I am her husband. She does not threaten divorce every time I do something to offend her. In fact, she has never threatened divorce and never will. We entered our marriage with the understanding that divorce would never be a possibility for us. That gives both of us much security in our relationship. I never have to worry about Staci walking out on me because I did something dumb.

While Staci will never divorce me when I offend her, my offenses do affect intimacy within our marriage. My sin hurts my wife, and her sin hurts me. Our sin strains our relationship until one of us asks forgiveness, and the other willingly grants forgiveness. For the sake of intimacy within our marriage, confession is necessary almost daily. When we are constantly confessing how we have offended each other and granting forgiveness for those offenses, we actually grow in intimacy. However, if we do not confess offenses quickly, and if we do not forgive quickly, intimacy wanes, and distance in our relationship grows.

Likewise, nothing can separate you from God's love. You are in a covenant relationship with Him, but sin will affect your intimacy with the Lord if you do not confess it. You sin daily, so daily you need to seek God's forgiveness. John writes,

> If we confess our sins, he is faithful and just to forgive us our sins and to cleanse us from all unrighteousness. (1 John 1:9)

If you confess your sin before God He will always forgive your sin. He never holds a grudge against you, and He never withholds His forgiveness. You will enjoy fellowship with God and growing intimacy with Him as you deal with your sin on a daily basis.

For the sake of your own soul, do not let sin hinder your walk with the Lord. When you fail to confess your sin, over time you will find yourself not desiring intimacy with God. I've seen it over and over again in the life of believers. I've seen believers so excited about their walk with the Lord and making progress in their spiritual growth. Then, all of a sudden something happens in their lives. Maybe they get caught up in something they know dishonors the Lord. Or, someone offends them, and they cannot forgive. They get eaten up with bitterness. Those believers who once craved intimacy with God no longer desire to spend time with other believers, spend time in God's Word, or spend time in prayer. I've seen sin destroy a believer's spiritual progress. The longer you dwell in your sin, the less you will crave intimacy with the

Lord. Thankfully, the more you grow in intimacy with the Lord the more you will also grow to hate sin just as God hates sin.

The problem is we are not as aware of our sin as God is. We live in a fallen world, and we have accepted sin as a normality of life. However, sin is not normal. Sin is an abnormality, a disease. Even though sin is not normal, we see it as a normal part of this world and our lives. We have never lived on a perfect earth with unhindered fellowship with the God of all creation. Because we are immersed in a sinful world, we have become immune to our own sin. Sin is simply not a big deal to many of us. We even rationalize it and excuse it. Since we are immune to the horror of our own sin, we need help seeing our sin so we might be able to confess it to the Lord and ask for His forgiveness. This is why David said to God:

> Search me, O God, and know my heart! Try me and know my thoughts! And see if there be any grievous way in me and lead me in the way everlasting! (Psalm 139:23-24)

We were not created for sin. Rather, God created us to live in an intimate relationship with Him, unstained by sin. When Christ returns, God will eradicate sin once and for all. He will recreate the earth, and sin will never have an influence on God's people again. We long for that day.

Many times we will pray something like, "God, I know I'm a sinner, and I ask that you forgive me of all my sins." While praying like that at best shows you realize you are a sinner; that kind of prayer doesn't really get to the heart of your problems. When someone you love has offended to you, you certainly do not want him to apologize to you by saying, "I'm sorry for all the bad things I've done to you." You want that person who has offended you to come clean with specific offenses he has committed against you. You want that person to know exactly what it is he did that hurt you, and you want him to acknowledge it, confess it, and not do it again. Don't you think this is what God desires as well when we confess our sins? Wouldn't it make sense that what He desires is not a blanket prayer which attempts to cover all of our sins? Instead, God desires specific confession of our rebellion with a sincere desire to repent.

If you are serious about intimacy with the Lord, and if you are serious about praying this petition in the Disciple's Prayer, you will make Psalm 139:23-24 a part of your daily prayer time. Daily ask God to search you, to search deep in the recesses of your soul and reveal to you anything at all that might be hindering you in your fellowship with Him.

Often times when we think of sin we think of the obvious things that offend God. We think of breaking one of the Ten Commandments or committing some kind of heinous crime. Some sins are easier to identify in our lives than others, but as you ask God to search your heart, you will find that the Holy Spirit will begin to reveal sins you don't think of often. The Holy Spirit will point out sins such as an ungrateful attitude or discontentment. He will show you your selfishness. He will show you your lack of self-control, your impatience, and your inability to control your anger. He will point out your bad attitude and the evil thoughts that you have towards others. He will point out your gossip, your slander, and your critical spirit. He will point out your jealousy and your wastefulness. To have God search your heart can be quite painful, but the pain is part of the refining process that God is working in you. It is difficult to see yourself for who you are, but the more God shows you who you are, the more amazing His grace will be to you. Be quick to seek God's forgiveness. Colossians 3:5 says, "Put to death therefore what is earthly in you..." As you seek God's forgiveness, His Spirit will help you put to death the sins that have hindered your relationship with Him.

3. *How does knowing you are in a covenant relationship with God affect your desire to obey Him?*

4. *Have you placed a priority on seeking God's forgiveness in your regular prayer times? Why or why not?*

5. *How have you seen sin hinder your intimacy with God? What has happened in your walk with the Lord when you have been slow to seek forgiveness?*

6. Do you regularly ask God to show you specific sins that are hindering your walk with Him? Why or why not? How can you make this a regular practice?

GRANTING FORGIVENESS

Notice that Jesus says, "Forgive us our debts *as we forgive our debtors*" (emphasis mine). The assumption is that a believer is a forgiving person. Faith in Christ makes you a forgiving person. You've been changed. You've experienced forgiveness from Almighty God for all of the sins that you have committed. How can you withhold forgiveness from someone who has not offended you as near as much as you have offended God? Right after the Disciple's Prayer Jesus says,

> For if you forgive others their trespasses, your heavenly Father will also forgive you, but if you do not forgive others their trespasses, neither will your Father forgive your trespasses. (Matthew 6:14-15)

Is Jesus saying that our forgiveness is contingent upon us being willing to forgive someone else? If so, does that mean we earn God's forgiveness by forgiving others?

Jesus' parable of the unforgiving servant helps us to understand what Jesus is communicating to us in Matthew 6:14-15. When Peter asked Jesus how many times he was supposed to forgive his brother when his brother offended him,

Jesus answered Peter by telling him this story in Matthew 18:23-35:

> Therefore the kingdom of heaven may be compared to a king who wished to settle accounts with his servants. When he began to settle, one was brought to him who owed him ten thousand talents. And since he could not pay, his master ordered him to be sold, with his wife and children and all that he had, and payment to be made. So the servant fell on his knees, imploring him, "Have patience with me, and I will pay you everything." And out of pity for him, the master of that servant released him and forgave him the debt. But when that same servant went out, he found one of his fellow servants who owed him a hundred denarii, and seizing him, he began to choke him, saying, "Pay what you owe." So his fellow servant fell down and pleaded with him, "Have patience with me, and I will pay you." He refused and went and put him in prison until he should pay the debt. When his fellow servants saw what had taken place, they were greatly distressed, and they went and reported to their master all that had taken place. Then his master summoned him and said to him, "You wicked servant! I forgave you all that debt because you pleaded with me. And should not you have had mercy on your fellow servant, as I had mercy on you?" And in anger his master delivered him to the jailers, until he should pay all his debt. So also my heavenly Father will do to every one of you, if you do not forgive your brother from your heart.

I imagine when Jesus told this story Peter was appalled by the actions of the wicked servant, and he should have been. Jesus told the story to demonstrate how absurd it would be for someone who has experienced such lavish grace to withhold grace from someone else. It simply doesn't make sense. For those of us who have experienced the grace of the Father, we will imitate His grace; maybe not perfectly, but a desire to imitate His grace will be evident. Therefore, if you are not willing to forgive someone who has hurt you, then you have not really experienced God's forgiveness. To put it bluntly, if you are not willing to forgive, you are not a child of God. God's children imitate their Father. You look most like your Father not when you attend church every Sunday or perform some kind of religious duty. Rather, you look most like your Father when you graciously extend mercy and forgiveness. If you are an unforgiving person, you are giving evidence that you have rejected the forgiveness of the Father. If you reject the forgiveness of the Father, He will reject you.

Several years ago, Riley Cooper was a NFL football player who played for the Philadelphia Eagles. He was caught on camera making a racial slur while attending a country music concert. The video immediately went viral, and Cooper was branded as a racist. He immediately apologized, and while his apology seemed sincere, his own teammates had mixed reactions to his apology. One Christian blogger contrasted the different reactions Cooper's teammates had to his apology. The blogger noted Michael Vick's response to Cooper's apology. Vick said,

> As a team we understood because we all make mistakes in life and we all do and say things that maybe we do mean and maybe we don't mean. But as a teammate I forgave him. We understand the magnitude of the situation. We understand a lot of people may be hurt and offended, but

> I know Riley Cooper. I've been with him for the last three years and I know what type of person he is. That's what makes it easy, and at the same time, hard to understand. But it's easy for me to forgive him.[1]

You might remember Michael Vick's legal troubles and the time he spent in prison after being found guilty of illegal dog fighting. After his imprisonment Vick experienced grace from the NFL. The NFL allowed him to resume his football career, and fans embraced him even after he committed heinous crimes. Vick experienced the power of forgiveness. Tchividjian also noted that Cooper's teammate LeSean McCoy had a different reaction than that of Vick's to Cooper's racial slur. McCoy said,

> I forgive him. We've been friends for a long time. But in a situation like this you really find out about someone. Just on a friendship level, I can't really respect someone like that...I guess the real him came out that day. The cameras are off, you don't think nobody's watching or listening, and then you find out who they really are. And to hear how he really came off, that shows you what he's really all about.[2]

McCoy had a completely different response than Vick. McCoy essentially said, "I forgive, but I don't forget." Comparing the two reactions to Cooper's transgression, The blogger writes,

> The difference between Vick and McCoy? Twenty-one months in a federal penitentiary and a deep knowledge of what it feels like to need forgiveness.[3]

When you have experienced forgiveness, how can you withhold forgiveness from someone else? I'm not sure of Vick's faith, but even if he is not a believer, he understands grace. How much more do those of us who are believers understand God's grace? Experiencing God's forgiveness makes us forgiving people.

How can you know if you have experienced the forgiveness of Christ in such a way that you desire to forgive others? Let me give you a few evidences of a forgiving person who has been changed by God's grace.

First, a forgiving person lives as if dead. Paul writes in Galatians 2:20,

> I have been crucified with Christ. It is no longer I who live, but Christ who lives in me. And the life I now live in the flesh I live by faith in the Son of God, who loved me and gave himself for me.

When someone offends you, your gut reaction is to think you have the right to be angry with the person who hurt you. However, if you have surrendered to Christ, you don't have any rights. You don't have the right to be angry. You don't have the right to retaliate, and you don't have the right to withhold forgiveness. You are dead to yourself. You are dead to the rights you think you have, and you are alive in Christ.

When someone hurts you, Christ commands you to forgive that person. It's really as simple as that. You can try to make excuses or give reasons as to why you can't forgive someone, but all of your excuses and reasons are inadequate. You need to do what Christ has called you to do. Obey Christ because you live for Him.

A second way you can know you are a forgiving person who has been forgiven by Christ is by examining your own heart. A forgiving person will be quick to recognize his or her own imperfections. You are far from perfect, and over the course of your life you have hurt many people. Why would you withhold forgiveness from someone when you have been just as guilty of hurting others yourself? Choosing to withhold forgiveness from someone else is quite hypocritical when you consider your own imperfections.

You might object immediately when you are challenged to forgive someone who has hurt you. You might say something like, "But you don't know how bad I've been hurt! You don't know the pain that I'm going through." I would never take your pain lightly, and if you are having a hard time forgiving someone, I know the depth of your hurt makes forgiving the person who hurt you seem like an impossibility. However, whenever forgiving someone seems impossible remember the forgiveness of our Lord. He was rejected by humanity. As He went to the cross He endured being spat upon, endless mockery, humiliation, and torturous beatings. Those who applauded His miracles and listened intently to His teachings turned on Him in His final moments. Although Jesus experienced rejection and humiliation, as He hung on the cross, He prayed to the Father, "Father, forgive them, for they know not what they do" (Luke 23:34).

Ultimately you need God's help in order to forgive. Apart from His help you cannot forgive like He does. When someone wrongs you, immediately take your hurt to the Lord. Maybe you should pray something like,

> *God, you know my hurt, and right now I cannot see past my hurt. I need your help. Help me see past my hurt so that I can forgive. Help me to see the person who hurt me as you see her. Help me not to carry bitterness. Rather, help me to be kind and tenderhearted just as you are kind and tenderhearted to me.*

If you will seek the Lord's help, you can be assured that He will give you the ability to forgive.

A third way to know you are a forgiving person who has been forgiven by Christ is examining your attitude toward those whom you say you have forgiven. Words are cheap. It is easy to say, "I forgive you." Maybe when you've told someone you forgive him, you say something like, "I forgive you, but I'll never forget what you've done to me." Is it real forgiveness to hold on to a grudge? When you make a statement like that essentially you are saying, "I'm saying the words, but the reality is I'm not forgiving you. I'm going to hold your sin over your head and remind you of the pain that you have caused me as often as I can."

As we've already discussed, God remembers your sin no more. In the same way, when you forgive, you are to remember the sin someone committed against you no more. I know it is impossible to forget what someone has done to you, but if you are going to imitate the forgiveness Christ has extended to you, you will treat the person who has sinned against you as if the sin never happened. Besides, if you hold on to grudges and become bitter, not only will you make the person who sinned against you miserable, but you will be miserable yourself. Why live in misery? Why not experience the freedom that comes in forgiving someone else? Why not restore relationships instead of allowing relationships to stay broken and destroyed?

Forgiveness requires that you trust God. You have to trust that His way is better than your way. You have to trust that imitating Him is always the wisest course of action. Forgiveness also requires selfless love. Isn't it true that one of the reasons we don't forgive is because we are just too in love with ourselves? We think we should be treated a certain way, and if we are mistreated, then whoever mistreats us must pay for how they mistreated us. The essence of self-love is to expect everyone else to bow and cater to you instead of you humbling yourself for the sake of others. Forgiveness requires that you love others, even those who hurt you, more than yourself. The only way to love those who hurt you is to immerse yourself in the God who loves you in spite of how you have grieved Him.

Praying this petition is difficult because this petition requires honesty and transparency. So you can walk in daily intimacy with God you must be willing to allow God to search your heart daily even if He might uncover sin you might not want to deal with. For the sake of your daily fellowship with Him, pray this petition daily. You might have someone in your life right now who has hurt you, and you are withholding forgiveness from that person because of the pain he or she caused you. Forgive that person. Your willingness to forgive is the evidence of a changed heart.

As you ask God to forgive you of your sins, also ask Him to give you a heart of forgiveness like His. Holding on to past offenses and bitterness will stifle not only your relationship with the person who has hurt you, it will also stifle your relationship with the Lord. Do not hold on to hurt any longer. Because of who you are in Christ, freely grant forgiveness to those who have hurt you. Maybe you have hurt someone. What is stopping you from confessing your offense to the person you have hurt and seeking his or her forgiveness? Do not let pride or selfishness hinder you from restoring relationships you have damaged. You will never regret choosing to forgive or asking for forgiveness, but you will often regret having an unforgiving heart.

7. Who have you not forgiven? What keeps you from granting forgiveness?

8. Who do you need to seek forgiveness from? What keeps you from seeking forgiveness?

9. How can the church better encourage others to grant and seek forgiveness?

10. How will your understanding of this petition change the way you pray?

[8]

Lord Protect Us

You need protection

FOR SOME REASON I used to have a tremendous fear of flying. I flew on a semi-regular basis, but every time I flew I feared the worst. My fear was so bad that every time I had an upcoming flight I would research the particular aircraft I was flying to see how many times that type of aircraft had crashed. When I was actually on a plane, I could not relax. Every time the plane made a noise I did not recognize, I assumed something was going wrong. Whenever I felt a little turbulence, I was sure the plane could not handle it. I imagined the slightest bit of turbulence was able to cause a plane to free fall out of the sky. I was fearful, and my fears were completely irrational.

As a pastor I began to lead international mission trips, which meant I would be on airplanes for hours at a time. I was absolutely terrified to fly across the Atlantic Ocean when

I led my first international mission trip, but something unexpected happened on that long flight. My fears went away. My only explanation for my fears being relieved is answered prayer. My fear of flying is completely gone, and now I love flying. I am able to relax on flights and enjoy the experience. My dream now is to take flying lessons and earn a private pilot certificate. I never thought that would be a dream of mine!

In one of the churches where I served as pastor, a gentleman who has been a private pilot for over forty years would occasionally take me up in his single-engine aircraft. Flying in that small plane was a completely different experience than flying in a huge commercial airliner, but it was so much fun! The first time we went flying my friend allowed me to take the controls once he got the plane to a certain altitude. I couldn't believe I was actually flying an airplane! It was exhilarating! Well, really, I was only steering the plane. My friend controlled the rudders and the throttle, and he kept a close eye on the instrument panel. He also kept a close eye on me. The plane had yokes on both sides of the aircraft. Even though I was controlling the yoke on the right side of the plane my friend was able to take control of the plane at any moment if I did something to put us in danger. My friend let me fly the plane, but he was there to protect me from myself. I flew the plane, but I am not a pilot. I needed protection, and there was not one moment as I steered the plane that I was not under the protection of a master pilot.

In the same way, as a believer, there is never a moment that you do not need protection. Mostly, you need protection from yourself. At any moment you are prone to give into temptation and rebel against God. You are weak, and you are easily influenced by the evil one. You will often find yourself in situations in which you can easily self-destruct. You need God's protection to keep you from rebelling against Him. In this last petition of the Disciple's Prayer Jesus teaches you to cry out to the Father for the spiritual protection you need so desperately.

"Lead us not into temptation" is an interesting request to ask of God, especially when you consider what James wrote in James 1:13,

> Let no one say when he is tempted, "I am being tempted by God," for God cannot be tempted with evil, and he himself tempts no one.

If God does not tempt anyone to sin, why would we ask Him not to lead us into temptation? Is it even possible for God to lead us into temptation?

The word translated *temptation* in our English bibles is an interesting word in the Greek language. The Greek word translated as *temptation* in Matthew 6:13 is also translated as *trial* or *test* in other passages of Scripture. When Bible translators translate from the Greek language to the English language they allow the context of the sentence to determine how to translate from one language to the other. For example, if you look again at James 1:13, the word *tempted* is the same Greek word that is also translated as *trials* in James 1:2-3 when James writes,

> Count it all joy, my brothers, when you meet trials of various kinds, for you know that the testing of your faith produces steadfastness.

However, James is communicating two different ideas in these two passages. In James 1:2-3, James teaches that trials are a natural and necessary part of the Christian faith. Your faith is going to be tested regularly. However, according to James 1:13, God will never entice you to evil. Satan, not God, will entice you to evil.

God will regularly test you. One of the most famous tests in the Bible is found in Genesis 22. Consider the nature of the test:

> After these things God tested Abraham and said to him, "Abraham!" And he said, "Here am I." He said, "Take your son, your only son Isaac, whom you love, and go to the land of Moriah, and offer him there as a burnt offering on one of the mountains of which I shall tell you." (Genesis 22:1)

Interestingly, the King James Version of the Bible records in Genesis 22:1, "And it came to pass after these things, that God did *tempt* Abraham..." (emphasis mine). Most modern translations are correct in recording that God tested Abraham rather than tempted, but the King James Version does help us to understand the nature of testing. God never entices us to sin. However, He regularly tests our faith, and in every test, a temptation to sin exists.

Let me explain what I mean. Genesis 22 is clearly a test of Abraham's faith to determine if he really trusted God. Abraham's life story is a remarkable story of the faithfulness of

God. Abraham and Sarah spent the majority of their adulthood childless. When Abraham was in his seventies, God promised Abraham he would have a child. From his child would come numerous descendants and a great nation that would be a blessing to the rest of the world. Abraham waited for God's promise to come to fruition. Finally, about twenty-five years later, when Abraham was one hundred-years-old, Sarah gave birth to a child. Isaac was the child God promised to Abraham, and you can imagine how much Abraham loved Isaac. Abraham and Sarah could not have been happier.

Did Abraham love Isaac more than God? Was Abraham more loyal to his son than to the God who gave him a son? Was Abraham's allegiance to his family or to the God of all creation? God tested Abraham to see where his loyalty really lay. Obviously, God knew before he tested Abraham where Abraham's allegiance lay. The test was for Abraham, not for God. God designed this test to show Abraham the extent of his faith.

The test was painful. Could you imagine God asking you to slaughter your beloved child on an altar? I imagine Abraham wrestled with what God called him to do. The night before he began his journey to Mount Moriah must have been a sleepless night as Abraham tossed and turned contemplating what God had commanded him to do. For three days Abraham traveled up the mountain with Isaac, and with every step he knew he was a step closer to killing his own son. I wonder on those two nights that Abraham and Isaac camped out on their way up Mount Moriah if Abraham stayed up watching his son sleep, crying and questioning if he had heard God correctly. Abraham did what God said. He tied his son down on an altar and raised a knife to kill him. Thankfully, as he raised his knife, God stopped him and said,

> Do not lay your hand on the boy or do anything to him, for now I know that you fear God, seeing you have not withheld your only son, from me. (Genesis 22:12)

Abraham passed the test. He had matured in his faith to the point that he trusted God even when God asked him to do what was seemingly impossible. God did not tempt Abraham. He did not entice him to evil. He tested Abraham, but within the test was a temptation. The temptation was to disobey God's direct command, and you can imagine the temptation was extremely enticing. I imagine as Abraham walked his son up Mount Moriah, Satan whispered in his ear, "Don't do this. God does not know what is best for you. Why would a loving God ask you to kill your son? What God is asking you to do is not logical."

While Satan may have whispered lies into Abraham's ears in an attempt to entice him, Abraham did not budge. He was resolute in his faith. He had seen the faithfulness of God over and over again, and he was not about to doubt God at this point in his life. Earlier in Abraham's faith journey, he might not have been as strong. A youthful, immature faith will often fall to temptation, but the more you grow in your faith the more you will trust God even during the most difficult tests. When God asked Abraham to sacrifice his son, Abraham had already been walking faithfully with the Lord for years. He was able to withstand the enemy and the temptation to disobey the Lord because of his faith in the God who had time and time again proven His faithfulness to him.

God will regularly test you as a means of refining your faith. Look back over the course of your Christian life, and you will see a series of tests. You will see various trials you have come through, and you will see how God was at work through your trials as He was teaching you more about Himself and also teaching you more about who you are. We need the tests. Tests are defining and refining moments in your walk with the Lord. The Apostle Peter wrote to a group of believers who experienced many tests. Each day these early believers faced persecution, but the persecution was God's means of refining their faith. Peter writes,

> In this you rejoice, though now for a little while, if necessary, you have been grieved by various trials, so that the tested genuineness of your faith—more precious than gold that perishes though it is tested by fire—may be found to result in praise and glory and honor at the revelation of Jesus Christ. (1 Peter 1:6-8)

God grew these believers through testing. As they were tested, they leaned into Christ and trusted Him more. God does the same thing in your life as well. He tests you to grow you.

Tests are good, but I am not ready for some tests because in every test is the temptation to disobey God. In some tests the temptation to disobey God is too overwhelming, and in my weakness I will disobey. For example, I'm not at the same place in my faith that Abraham was in his faith when God asked him to sacrifice Isaac. If God tested my faith by asking me to slaughter my son on an altar (not that He would) I would fail that test. In that test the temptation to disobey God would be overwhelming, and I would disobey. I would listen to my voice rather than the voice of God.

In every test is the temptation to allow Satan to influence me to follow my desires rather than the Spirit of God. James writes,

> But each person is tempted when he is lured and enticed by his own desire. Then desire when it has conceived gives birth to sin, and sin when it is fully grown brings forth death. (James 1:14-15)

In every test I can either surrender my desires to Christ and follow His will, or I can give in to the temptation to reject God's will and follow after my own desires. In every test that God gives me, this temptation will be present. God did not cause the temptation. The temptation is the result of my sinful flesh. I'm weak, and I'm at war with myself. In the midst of my temptation I desperately need God's protection. I need Him to protect me from my own selfish desires. I need Him to protect me from the lies of the enemy who is whispering in my ear, "What God is asking you to do is not logical. Do what you desire instead."

In the Disciple's Prayer Jesus is calling us to acknowledge our weakness and ask God for protection. We are weak, and we are not ready for some tests. However, with God's help, as we cry out to Him, He will give us the strength to pass any test. Paul writes,

> No temptation has overtaken you that is not common to man. God is faithful, and he will not let you be tempted beyond your ability, but with the temptation he will also provide the way of escape, that you may be able to endure it. (1 Corinthians 10:13)

This passage of Scripture is misquoted so often by many well-meaning believers. You've probably heard someone say, or maybe you've said yourself, "God will never give you more than you can handle." That statement is a sloppy misinterpretation of 1 Corinthians 10:13. The passage doesn't teach that God will never give you more than you can handle. God often will give you more than you can handle. In my own life I cannot pinpoint anything I can handle without God. The entirety of my life is more than I can handle, and I desperately need God's help.

Paul's point is that God helps you in your tests. In every test you take, you need God's help. A mature Christian knows she must depend on the empowerment of the Holy Spirit to overcome the temptation to disobey God in the midst of testing. Never forget you are weak. In your own strength you will fail many tests by giving into temptation, thus demonstrating your need for God to continue to grow you in your faith. When a test is overwhelming, and you are tempted to disobey, cry out to God. Cry out to God when your faith is weak. He will help you. He is the way of escape!

The cross proves that God is our way of escape. At the cross, our Father provided us a way to be free from the penalty and power of sin by allowing His Son to die in our place and rising three days later so we might know our victory over temptation and sin is in Christ alone. While you might be tempted, as you cry out for God's help, you can trust God will protect you from the temptation to follow your desires rather than submit to His will. The death and resurrection of His Son proves that He is the only one you can trust to protect you from temptation.

How then do we practically ask God to "lead us not into temptation"? You know your weaknesses. Perhaps you have struggled with gossip. Maybe for you, praying this petition means asking God to keep you from those people who have a tendency to gossip. Maybe you struggle with lust. Perhaps you should ask God to keep you from watching television shows or viewing internet sites that will lead you to lust. Ask Him to fill your mind with thoughts of His kingdom rather than images that will entice lust. Maybe your test is that you've lost your job, and you are tempted to worry about how you are going to take care of your needs rather than trusting God to provide. Ask God to lead you to passages of Scripture that will assure you of His faithfulness and ask Him to help you remember all the times in your life when He's been faithful to you.

Asking God to lead you not into temptation is to ask God to protect you from your tendency to disobey God when testing comes. It's asking God to protect you from the sins you are so easily prone to commit. Testing will come, and you will be tempted in your tests. The enemy will influence you to choose to rebel against God. Pray for God's protection, and He will help you to walk in faith even in the midst of your most difficult tests.

1. How has God tested your faith? Did you pass or fail? What have you learned from those tests?

2. In the tests that you have experienced, what were the temptations that arose? Were you able to overcome? If so, how?

3. How is God your way of escape in temptation? How can your knowledge of the death and resurrection of Christ help you to overcome temptation?

4. How can you more effectively pray for others who are struggling with temptation?

5. In those areas you are weak, how should you pray for God not to lead you into temptation?

GOD IS YOUR PROTECTOR AND DELIVERER

We struggle with temptation because we are at war. We are at war with ourselves. While we are in the process of daily crucifying our flesh, remnants of our old sinful ways still tempt us and entice us to dishonor the Lord. Also, an enemy exists. Satan is our adversary who, in our moments of testing, attempts to influence us to rebel against the God who loves us. Peter writes,

> Be sober-minded; be watchful. Your adversary the devil prowls around like a roaring lion, seeking someone to devour. Resist him, firm in your faith, knowing that the same kinds of suffering are being experienced by your brotherhood throughout the world. (1 Peter 5:8-9)

Jesus teaches us to ask the Father to deliver us from the evil one. Some modern Bible translations record Jesus saying, "deliver us from evil," but ultimately evil comes from the original rebel who tempted Eve in the garden: Satan himself.

We live in a church culture that by and large chooses to ignore Satan. Our modern images of Satan with a pitchfork and pointy tail have made the whole idea of Satan seem ludicrous. However, simply because we do not want to talk about the reality of Satan does not mean he does not exist. Satan is real, and he is seeking to devour you. His tactics to destroy you are varied. My friend, you are in a very real war, and Satan is a very real enemy who desires to see you destroyed. Paul described the reality of the war we are fighting. In Ephesians 6:12 Paul writes,

> For we do not wrestle against flesh and blood, but against the rulers, against the authorities, against the cosmic powers over this present darkness, against the spiritual forces of evil in the heavenly places.

You are at war with the enemy, but the war you are fighting is different than any other war that has ever been fought. According to Paul, the war you are fighting is different because you are fighting against spiritual forces, but the war is also different because you are not fighting *for* victory. Rather, you are fighting *from* victory. You are already victorious over Satan. You have already been delivered from the hands of the enemy. When Jesus Christ rose from the dead, your victory was secured.

If you have already been delivered from the enemy, then why does Jesus teach us to ask God for protection and deliverance from the enemy? While Satan is defeated, he has not yet experienced his final sentencing. His final sentencing to an eternity in the lake of fire will happen at the end of time (Revelation 12:10). In the meantime, our enemy roams the earth, knowing he is defeated and his eternal punishment is imminent, but Satan is not going down without a fight. He's going down swinging, and his goal is to torment God's people as he goes down.

While he might torment us, and while he might influence us to rebel against our Father, he will never overcome us. Jesus' death and resurrection rendered Satan absolutely powerless over our eternal salvation. Speaking of the finished work of Christ, the writer of Hebrews writes,

> Since therefore the children share in flesh and blood, he himself likewise partook of the same things, that through death he might destroy the one who has the power of death, that is, the devil, and deliver all those who through fear of death were subject to lifelong slavery. (Hebrews 2:14-15)

Satan might influence you to sin against God, but he can never take away the salvation that God has given you. If you have surrendered to Christ, you are no longer a slave to the enemy. You are securely in God's family. However, this does not mean Satan is not going to attack you. Scripture records a number of ways that Satan attacks us and attempts to cause us to take our eyes off of Jesus. Satan attacks by accusing us. The Bible often refers to Satan as the devil. Our English word *devil* comes from the Greek word *diablos* which means *slanderer* or *accuser*. Satan constantly accuses us and reminds us of our shortcomings. He constantly goes before the Father and points out our flaws. John writes,

> And I heard a loud voice in heaven saying, Now the salvation and the power and the kingdom of our God and the authority of his Christ have come, for the accuser of our brothers has been thrown down, who accuses them day and night before our God." (Revelation 12:10)

Thankfully, our Father does not listen to the accusations of the enemy, and neither should you. Certainly, Jesus convicts us of our sin, but He doesn't accuse us. Instead, He advocates for us (1 John 2:1). On the other hand, the accuser will often whisper lies into your ear like, "You will never be good enough in the eyes of God. You will never be able to overcome that sin you struggle with. God will never be pleased with you." Do not believe the accusations. God's acceptance of you and His love for you are not based on anything you have done or haven't done. God loves you simply because He chooses to love you, and Jesus has already pleased the Father on your behalf. Do not let the accusations of the enemy cause you to wallow in self-pity and take your eyes off of who you are in Christ.

Satan also seeks to devour us through other means. Jesus called Satan the father of all lies (John 8:44). Satan lies to God's children by raising up false teachers who twist the Word of God. False teachers might use Scripture and might even make some accurate claims about Christ, but their deception leads people away from the truth of Christ rather than to the truth of Christ. Paul writes,

> See to it that no one takes you captive by philosophy and empty deceit, according to human tradition, according to the elemental spirits of the world, and not according to Christ. (Colossians 2:8)

Through lies, false teaching, and temptation, Satan entices believers away from the Lord. Satan disguises his demonic influence well. He has a way of making his lies look like truth and evil temptations look like righteousness. Paul warns the church at Corinth about the deceptive nature of Satan and his servants.

> ...for even Satan disguises himself as an angel of light. So it is no surprise if his servants, also, disguise themselves as servants of righteousness. Their end will correspond to their deeds. (2 Corinthians 11:14-15)

Yes, Satan is a defeated foe. His eternal punishment is imminent, and, yes, he will never be able to snatch you out of God's hand. However, he will come after you daily. He will torment you. He will tempt you. He will try to convince you to turn your back on the God who loves you. He's a powerful force, but you have someone much more powerful than Satan living inside of you. God has placed the Holy Spirit in you, and you can trust that God's Spirit will protect you and deliver you from the daily attacks of the enemy if you will submit to Him. James writes, "Submit yourselves therefore to God. Resist the devil, and he will flee from you" (James 4:7). As you submit to the Lord, He will protect you by empowering you to be able stand against the devil. If you are walking in the power of God, the devil simply cannot stand against you. God has already delivered you from Satan. You are victorious over him. He cannot take away what God has already given you, and God gives you daily deliverance from the attacks of your defeated foe as you submit to the Lord.

God has given you everything you need to battle the enemy. You have been given the full armor of God. Paul describes the armor of God in Ephesians 6:13-17.

> Therefore take up the whole armor of God, that you may be able to withstand in the evil day, and having done all, to stand firm. Stand therefore, having fastened on the belt of truth, and having put on the breastplate of righteousness, and, as shoes for your feet, having put on the readiness given by the gospel of peace. In all circumstances take up the shield of faith, with which you can extinguish all the flaming darts of the evil one; and take the helmet of

salvation, and the sword of the Spirit, which is the word of God...

I have found it helpful to pray through this passage of Scripture. I know that I am always facing spiritual warfare. As a pastor, I am more sensitive to the reality of spiritual warfare before I stand before God's people to preach the Word of God. In those moments as I enter the pulpit and begin to speak the Word of God, I look out over my congregation and I can feel the battle that is raging in the hearts and lives of the people to whom I minister. In those moments that I am preaching the Word of God I am keenly aware of my dependency on God's power and protection.

On those days that I am more acutely aware of Satan's influence, I pray something like,

> God, I thank you that you have given me all I need to stand against the enemy. You have given me truth. You are the truth, and your truth has set me free. Help me to walk in truth today. I thank you that you have given me righteousness. I am far from righteous, but as a gift, you have given me the righteousness of Christ. Help me to walk today in His righteousness. I thank you that you have given me a message to proclaim. I know proclaiming the Gospel message will be difficult, and I will face persecution for speaking your Gospel message. I also know that all who respond to your message will experience peace. Help me to walk in your peace and help me to point people to the peace they can have in Christ. I thank you for the gift of faith. I ask that you strengthen my faith, and I pray that today my trust in you would be my shield against the attacks of the enemy. Help me today to trust your word rather than trusting the lies of Satan. Thank you for my salvation. Thank you that because of the salvation you have given me, you are now renewing my mind. Protect my mind

today. Help me not to entertain thoughts of the enemy. Thank you for your Word. Thank you that your word is my sword. Help me today to learn from your Word so that when the enemy does attack I will be able to easily remember Scripture so I can diffuse His lies with your truth.

Meditating on and praying through Scripture like Ephesians 6:13-17 will help you in your daily battle with the enemy. Know that you will battle the enemy until the day that Christ calls you home. Some days you will lose the battle. You will let your guard down. You will not put on the full armor of God. While you might lose some battles along the way, you will never be eternally defeated, and the more you grow in intimacy with Christ, the more battles you will win. You will never be perfect in this life, but you will see more and more victories as you mature in your faith.

Realize that the only way you will win the battle is on your knees. You do not have the power in and of yourself to stand against the enemy, but God does. God freely gives you power to stand against the enemy as you cry out to Him in submission and ask for His help in the battle. Do not neglect to pray for His protection and His deliverance. You need it. Your life will be a series of tests, and the way you respond to temptation in the midst of your testing will reveal the maturity of your faith. God is your help in your testing, and God is your power against the devil's schemes.

Notice this petition, like the others, is plural. We are to pray for the protection of each other. The Disciple's Prayer forces us to remember that all who follow Christ are one in Him. One person's struggle with sin will affect the entire body of Christ. We must pray for those who are weak and easily swayed by the enemy. Regretfully, we have more of a tendency to gossip about those who are weak in the faith rather than pray for them. The body of Christ will be ineffective in its witness when people are being easily influenced by the enemy. The best way you can minister to those in your congregation who are struggling with sin is to pray for them. Pray regularly for God's deliverance and protection for those you know struggle with temptation.

6. *Do you acknowledge that Satan is a real influence or do you ignore his influence? What is the danger of ignoring his influence?*

7. *How does knowing that you fight from victory instead of for victory give you hope as you battle demonic influences?*

8. *Evaluate your prayer life. How often do you pray for God's protection and deliverance from the evil one?*

9. *How will knowing that Satan is a real influence who seeks to devour God's people change the way you pray for yourself? For others?*

[9]
Now What?

WE HAVE DISCUSSED THE Disciple's Prayer phrase by phrase, but what do you do with all you have learned about this model prayer? How do you practically use the Disciple's Prayer in your own life so your prayer time might be more effective? Should you always pray through the Disciple's Prayer phrase by phrase when you pray? In this final chapter, I want to give you some practical suggestions as you develop a more effective prayer life. Know I am learning just like you. I do not profess to be a graduate of the school of prayer. I have much to learn, but I do want to share some insights that have been helpful for me as I have grown in my own prayer life.

Discipline Yourself to Pray

If you want to succeed in any area of life, you must have a plan of action. This is true of prayer as well. If you want to be more effective in your prayer life, you have to plan to spend time with the Lord. You must discipline yourself to pray. Consider what Paul writes about the role of discipline in a believer's life.

> Do you not know that in a race all the runners run, but only one receives the prize? So run that you may obtain it. Every athlete exercises self-control in all things. They do it to receive a perishable wreath, but we an imperishable. So I do not run aimlessly; I do not box as one beating the air. But I discipline my body and keep it under control, lest after preaching to others I myself should be disqualified. (1 Corinthians 9:24-27)

I've never been much of an athlete but growing up I did play a good bit of baseball. I remember throwing the ball with my dad in the backyard after he got home from work in the afternoons. My dad was an excellent baseball player as a younger man, and he worked with me to teach me as much as he could. While I wasn't the best baseball player, the more I practiced, the better I became. Paul compares followers of Christ to athletes. Like an excellent athlete, a Christ-follower disciplines his spiritual body to bring it into conformity with God's will. Regarding prayer, the more you discipline yourself to spend time in God's presence, the more you will find yourself being conformed to the will of God.

Paul encouraged Timothy to train himself for godliness (1 Timothy 4:8). When it comes to your walk with the Lord, what's your training program? Are you disciplining yourself to pray? The word discipline sounds negative because it implies work. Who wants to work at his walk with the Lord? We expect everything in our spiritual life to come naturally and without any effort. After all, isn't our spiritual growth ultimately a work of God?

Ultimately your spiritual growth is a work of God (Philippians 1:6), but you must cooperate with the work of the Spirit. You have to surrender daily to the Spirit of God and give Him free reign to work within you. You are not without responsibility in your spiritual growth. You must discipline yourself to spend time in God's presence and pray with a heart of surrender so you might experience the Holy Spirit growing you in Christ.

If you are not careful, disciplining yourself to pray can be nothing more than a practice in legalism. If the goal of disciplining yourself to set aside consistent time to pray is so you can feel good about yourself for making prayer a daily habit, then you've missed the point of praying. If the goal of daily prayer is so you can check off some kind of spiritual checklist in an attempt to show God how spiritual you are, you are in danger of being just like the Pharisees. The Pharisees were extremely disciplined, but they weren't training themselves in godliness. The goal of disciplining yourself to pray is to put yourself in a position in which you can be changed continually by the Spirit of God. Prayer is one of God's primary ordained means to conform His children to His will. The more you discipline yourself to be in God's presence with a heart of surrender and desire God to change you as you spend time with Him, the more you will be conformed to His will. Don't discipline yourself so you can feel good about a spiritual habit you've developed. Discipline yourself to pray so that God might make you more like His Son.

We already saw Jesus' prayer strategy in the first chapter. His plan was to rise every morning to spend time with the Father. I already know you might be thinking. "I'm not a morning person!" Maybe you're thinking, "I already get up at 5:00 a.m. to get myself ready for work, then I have to get the kids up and off to school before I have to be at work by 8:00 a.m." I don't know your schedule, and your schedule may present some challenges for you to start your day in communion with God. Let me encourage you to do whatever you can to adjust your schedule to begin your day with the Lord. You will not regret beginning your day with uninterrupted time with your Father.

You might be thinking, "Well, why can't I set aside time in the evening to spend with the Lord." You can, and I would encourage you to set aside time in the evening to spend with the Lord. In our home, the evening is a good time to pray together as a family, but just in my experience, the evening is not the best time for me to have uninterrupted time alone with the Lord for a couple of reasons. First, I want to give time to my family in the evening. My time with my wife and child is precious as well, and I do not want to isolate myself from them in the evening. I want to minister to them. Second, my mind is not as sharp in the evening. I do not think as clearly after a long day of work as I do when I rise early in the morning. Also, when I begin my day with time with the Lord I am able to say, "Lord, today belongs to you. Help me to be sensitive to your Spirit throughout the day." For me, starting my day with time with the Lord sets the tone of my whole day.

Ultimately, we shouldn't be legalistic about when to set aside uninterrupted time with the Lord. I know a variety of exceptions exist. For example, a shift worker starts his day in the evening rather than the morning, and some people are night owls and have a much sharper mind in the evening. I understand God has wired us all differently, but I do think there is wisdom in imitating the prayer life of Jesus as much as possible. However, the most important thing is to be consistent and disciplined in your time with the Lord. Set an appointment with God and keep it. I know you'll be praying throughout the day as different situations arise, but uninterrupted time with God is essential to your spiritual growth.

1. How disciplined is your prayer life? How has reading this book challenged you to be more disciplined in your prayer life?

2. What will be your plan to spend time with the Lord on a regular basis? Who will hold you accountable as you seek to grow in your time with the Lord? How will that person hold you accountable?

Use the Disciple's Prayer as a Starting Point

Should you pray through the Disciple's Prayer phrase by phrase every day? Obviously, you can pray to God in a variety of ways. You don't necessarily have to pray phrase by phrase through the Disciple's Prayer, but this is the model prayer in which Jesus teaches us to pray. If you are just starting to learn to pray, I would suggest you begin by praying through the Disciple's Prayer phrase by phrase each day. As you discipline yourself to pray phrase by phrase through the Disciple's Prayer, you will find yourself growing in your ability to communicate freely to the Lord. Jesus has given you a blueprint that clearly shows you how to build an effective prayer life. Why not follow the blueprint that He has laid out for you?

This doesn't mean you simply repeat the Disciple's Prayer as a ritual, but rather you think through each phrase as you come before the presence of the Father. As you begin your time of prayer, think about what it means that God is your Father. How should knowing He is your Father affect the way you approach God in your prayers?

As you pray, spend time hallowing God's name. Begin to praise God for who He is and what He has done for you. Thank God for the blessings He has given you. Reflect on your salvation and where you would be if it were not for Christ. Praise Him for your salvation. Simply spend time worshipping the Lord. You would be amazed at how much time you could spend simply reflecting on the character and nature of God and praising Him as a response to His greatness.

After hallowing God's name, move on to praying for the kingdom of God. Ask God to help you live as a citizen of His kingdom here on earth. Daily ask God to help you surrender to His lordship. Ask for His help to be effective in sharing the good news of the kingdom with others. Ask Him to help you intentionally invest in the lives of others. Pray by name for believers you know in your small group or Sunday School class. Pray God would use them to be effective in their Gospel witness. Pray for your church. Pray that your church would be surrendered to the purpose of God's kingdom and pray for your church to be effective in expanding the kingdom throughout the earth. Pray for missionaries, pastors, and others who are laboring for the sake of the Gospel. Pray for your lost family members and friends. Pray for the return of Christ. After all, we long for the day that Christ will return and reign as king over all once and for all. Ask God to give you a desire to see the King of kings return and rule over this earth.

Pray for God's will to be done on earth as in heaven. Ask God to help you to align your life to His will. His will is for you to worship Him with everything you are. Ask for His help to worship Him in spirit and truth. Ask God to conform your character to the character of Christ. Ask Him to change everything about you; your actions, your thoughts, and your attitudes so you might be brought into conformity with His will. Ask God to give you a desire to do whatever it is He asks of you with joy.

Pray for your daily needs. Thank God that He is your provider and ask Him to give you exactly what you need for the day to accomplish His will. Ask Him to help you be content with whatever it is He gives you. Pray for the needs of others. Pray for those you know who are ill and need God's strength to sustain them through their illness. Pray for those you know who have other physical needs and ask God how He might use you to meet the needs of others. Would He have you be an answer to someone else's prayer?

Ask God to search your heart and reveal to you any sin that is hindering your fellowship with Him. Ask God to forgive each sin that comes to mind and ask His Spirit to help you turn from that sin and walk in obedience to His Word. Ask God to bring to mind any ways you have hurt or offended others and ask Him to help you seek their forgiveness. If anyone has hurt you, ask God to help you not to become bitter, and ask Him to help you forgive the one who has hurt you.

Ask God to protect you from evil. If you are facing difficulties and trials, ask God to help you keep your eyes focused on Him so you might not give into temptation in the midst of your testing. Ask God to help you clearly see the lessons He wants you to learn as you walk through difficult times. Ask for His wisdom as you go through trials so you might know how to respond to your trials with the mind of Christ. Ask Him to guard your heart from disobedience and ask Him to help you put on the full armor of God so you might be able to stand firm against the enemy.

When the Disciple's Prayer is the model for your prayer life you will have plenty to pray about. As you pray through the Disciple's Prayer you will find yourself spending more and more time in God's presence as you use each petition to help guide your conversation with God. The goal of prayer is not to see how long you can pray but using the Disciple's Prayer as a model for your own prayer life will help you to avoid praying short, superficial prayers that fail to build intimacy with the Father.

The Disciple's Prayer is where you start as you learn how to pray. As you grow in your prayer life you probably won't find it necessary to pray through the Disciple's Prayer phrase by phrase, carefully thinking about how you might pray through each petition. Instead, after you have disciplined yourself to pray through these petitions you will find yourself naturally praying through these petitions whenever you spend time with the Lord.

3. How do you think using the Disciple's Prayer as a starting point will help you grow in your prayer life?

4. Which petition do you think will be the most challenging for you to pray? Why?

Pray with an Open Bible

How does God speak to His children? Hebrews 1:1-2 clearly states that God speaks to us through His Son.

> Long ago, at many times and in many ways, God spoke to our fathers by the prophets, but in these last days he has spoken to us by his Son, whom he appointed the heir of all things, through whom also he created the world.

In John 1:1, the Gospel writer explains to us that Jesus is the very Word of God. Jesus is the voice of the Father. How do we hear the voice of Jesus? Perhaps you have heard someone say, "Prayer is just as much about hearing God speak as it is speaking to God yourself." If you want to hear the voice of Jesus, do you sit quietly in a room with closed eyes and folded hands and wait to hear His voice? Does the risen Lord speak to us in the silence of meditation?

Our Savior can speak to us any way He wants. Sometimes He does choose to speak to us through our thoughts or through the counsel of other people, but when He does speak to us His voice will never contradict His written Word. While our Lord may at times speak to us through our inner thoughts or other people, He primarily chooses to communicate to us through the written Word. The Bible is God's written Word which reveals the living Word, Jesus Christ. Every page of Scripture points us to Jesus.

After the resurrection, two men were on their way to Emmaus when they encountered the risen Lord. On their journey to Emmaus, Jesus took time to explain to these travelers how all of Scripture points to Him. Luke records,

> And beginning with Moses and all the Prophets, he interpreted to them in all the Scriptures the things concerning himself. (Luke 24:27)

If you want to hear the voice of Christ, you must go to the Bible because all of the Bible is about Him! The Bible explains how to know Jesus, walk with Jesus, and honor Jesus.

The Bible is not an ancient book with little relevance for our lives. In the Bible we hear the voice of our Lord as He teaches us through the human authors of Scripture how we are to live in the center of His will for His glory. If the Bible is the primary way that our Lord speaks to us, wouldn't it make sense to pray with an open Bible, expecting to hear God speak to you from His Word as you prayerfully study His Word?

Let me suggest to you a couple of ways to pray through the Disciple's Prayer with an open Bible. One way is to make a list of Bible verses to meditate on for each petition in the Disciple's Prayer. Start with the opening address, "Our Father." What does the Bible have to say about God as your Father? Find as many passages as you can in the Old and New Testaments that speak of God as Father. How do these verses describe God as Father? What do these verses say about the character and nature of God as Father? How do these passages of Scripture help your understanding of God as your Father? As you read these Scriptures that express the Fatherhood of God, and as you thank God for adopting you as His child, He is going to speak to you. You are going to hear His still, small voice comforting you and gently reminding you that because He is your Father you can trust Him with your life.

Move on to the petitions of the Disciple's Prayer. What does the Bible say about hallowing God's name? You can make a long list of verses calling you to worship God for His greatness. What does the Bible say about God's kingdom and His will? What does the Bible say about God's provisions? What does the Bible say about God's forgiveness? What does God say about the role of testing and temptation in a believer's life? Grab a Bible concordance and simply make a list of as many Bible verses as you can that speak to each of the petitions of the Disciple's Prayer. As you discipline yourself to pray through the Disciple's Prayer, reflect on the verses you discovered. You might want to take time simply to think through a couple of different Bible passages pertaining to a particular petition each day. As you think about these Bible passages as they relate to each petition of the Disciple's Prayer, you will hear God's voice as He teaches you more about His character and His will.

A second way of praying through the Disciple's Prayer with an open Bible is to pray through the petitions of the Lord's Prayer as you systematically read through the Bible. While examining the Bible to discover Bible passages relating to the petitions of the Disciple's Prayer is a helpful way to pray with your Bible open, nothing takes the place of systematically reading and praying through the Bible. Make a plan for Bible reading. You might plan to read through the entire Bible over the course of a year, or maybe your plan is to read through the New Testament several times over the course of a year. Perhaps you desire to focus on the Gospels for several months. Regardless, make a plan to read through Scripture systematically.

Don't just read the Bible simply for the sake of being able to say you've read through the Bible. Read through the Bible with the expectation that God will speak to you as you prayerfully read His Word. I find it helpful to pray something like this when I begin my Bible reading:

> Lord I know this is your Word, and I know you desire to speak to me through your Word. Help me to listen carefully for your voice as I read.

As I read verse by verse, I'm carefully thinking about how God's Word affects my life and speaks to situations I am facing. As I'm reading, I'm also thinking about how the particular passage of Scripture I'm reading aids me in praying a specific petition of the Disciple's Prayer.

For example, if I'm reading Genesis 1, that passage is going to lead me to hallow God's name. If I'm reading the story of Adam and Eve's sin, it's going to lead me to search my own heart for unconfessed sin so I can seek God's forgiveness for a particular sin I have committed. If I'm reading the story of Jesus' encounter with Nicodemus in John 3 or the story of the Prodigal Son in Luke 15, I'm going to be led to pray for those who are lost, or the advancement of God's kingdom. If I'm studying Galatians 5, I'm going to ask God for His will to be done in my life as I ask Him to develop the fruit of the Spirit within me.

As I systematically read Scripture, listening for God's voice in its pages, I'm allowing Scripture to fuel the way I pray the different petitions of the Disciple's Prayer. I'm always amazed at how God leads me to pray as I think prayerfully through what I'm reading in His Word, and I'm always amazed at how reading His Word naturally leads me to pray in concert with the petitions of the Disciple's Prayer. I'm also amazed at how God speaks to me through the process. As I'm prayerfully considering His Word, God's Spirit ministers to me, gives me guidance in different areas of my life, and constantly reminds me to put all of my hope in Jesus no matter my circumstances.

These are things I have found helpful in my own prayer life, but I hesitate to tell you, "This is the way you must pray!" You might discover other ways to cultivate intimacy with God through prayer. As you grow in your prayer life, God will continue to reveal Himself to you in a variety of ways, and you will develop your own patterns of prayer. I hope these suggestions will give you some guidance as you learn how to spend time with your Father. Understand that reading God's Word and prayer go hand in hand. I strongly discourage your from separating one from the other.

5. If you are reading this book with a small group or a friend, take some time to search the Scriptures together to discover different Bible passages that inform your understanding and fuel your prayers for each petition of the Disciple's Prayer.

6. Do you prayerfully read through the Bible? If you are studying this material with a small group or a friend, share your plan for reading Scripture over the next few months. How do you think prayerfully reading through the Bible will change the way you communicate with God?

Remember the Ultimate Goal of Prayer

You might be a bit overwhelmed as you finish this book. You might think you will never be able to pray like Jesus teaches. It might seem overwhelmingly time-consuming, tedious, and intense. To be sure, prayer is hard work. It does take discipline, but as you begin to make daily communication with God a more regular part of your life, you will see growth. Stick with it and don't give up.

Praying the way Jesus teaches us how to pray requires a commitment of time. There's simply no way around the time commitment prayer requires. Just like any other relationship you have, your relationship with the Lord is an investment of time. As you invest time into knowing Him, you will find your relationship with Him deepening. I would encourage you to set goals. Maybe you can set a goal of praying for ten minutes a day for the next few weeks. You might find that setting a goal of praying ten minutes a day will only give you enough time to pray through one or two petitions in the

Lord's Prayer. Make it your goal to pray through all of the petitions of the Disciple's Prayer over the course of a week, praying through one or two petitions a day.

After you have established a routine of daily prayer, gradually increase the time you spend in prayer each day until you find yourself consistently praying through the petitions of the Disciple's Prayer. Do not get discouraged when you miss a day or two of spending time with the Lord. Simply start again and be consistent. The Lord will honor your discipline, and you will never regret your time spent with the Lord.

While prayer requires a commitment of time, beware of the temptation to turn prayer into a task. If you are not careful, prayer can become just another item on your daily to-do list. Again, if you turn prayer into simply a daily task, the goal of prayer will be no more than the satisfaction of patting yourself on the back for being a good, disciplined Christian. You'll miss the goal of prayer entirely.

The ultimate goal of prayer is always life change. We often approach prayer in an attempt to change God's mind and bend Him to our will, but God invites us to communicate with Him so He might change us. In his famous devotional book, *My Utmost for His Highest*, Oswald Chambers writes,

> To say that "prayer changes things" is not as close to the truth as saying, "Prayer changes me and then I change things." God has established things so that prayer, on the basis of redemption, changes the way a person looks at things. Prayer is not a matter of things externally, but one of working miracles in a person's inner nature.[1]

The goal of the Christian life, not only prayer, is to be changed by the Spirit of God so we might become more and more like Christ. As you spend time with the Father with a desire for Him to change you, He will. He will grow you in your love for Him, and He will make you more and more like Christ. As you pray, God may not change your circumstances and make them more favorable for you, but He will change your perspective on your circumstances. He will show you how to respond to unfavorable circumstances in a way that honors Christ.

In 2 Corinthians 12, the Apostle Paul admitted he was having an issue that he continually prayed about but found no relief. Paul had a "thorn in the flesh." Bible scholars are uncertain of the specifics of Paul's thorn in the flesh. Some scholars believe his thorn was some type of nagging, physical ailment that greatly hindered him. Other scholars believe his thorn was perhaps a certain individual who tormented Paul and tried to make his life miserable. Regardless of what his thorn was, Paul begged the Lord to take it from him. Paul writes, "Three times I pleaded with the Lord about this, that it should leave me" (2 Corinthians 12:8).

The Lord didn't remove Paul's thorn, but as Paul continued to seek the Father concerning his thorn, God began to do a work within Paul. God did not change Paul's circumstances, but He changed Paul's outlook on his circumstances. Paul recognized his thorn in the flesh was used by God to keep him humble. Paul writes,

> So to keep me from becoming conceited because of the surpassing greatness of the revelations, a thorn was given

me in the flesh, a messenger of Satan to harass me, to keep me from becoming conceited. (2 Corinthians 12:7)

Not only did Paul's thorn in the flesh keep him humble, Paul was also convinced that God gave him this thorn in the flesh to remind him that His grace was sufficient. The thorn might have weakened Paul, but it did not render his God powerless. Rather, the thorn helped Paul depend on the power of God in his human weakness (2 Corinthians 12:9). Prayer changed Paul. Three times he pleaded with the Lord, and in those three times of pleading with the Lord over whatever ailed Him, God changed Paul's heart toward his ailment. I am sure as Paul learned more about God's grace in the midst of his affliction, he fell more in love with his Lord.

Allow prayer to change you by approaching God with a desire to be changed. If you approach God with a selfish and hard heart, you will never experience the life change and growing intimacy with God that He so desires for you. As we've seen repeatedly, this is why the Disciple's Prayer is so beautiful and helpful. If you use the Disciple's Prayer as a model for your own prayer life, it will be difficult for your prayers to be anything other than centered on God's will. The Disciple's Prayer is God-centered, not man-centered, and in this prayer Jesus has taught us a way to pray that accomplishes the goal of prayer. If you consistently pray in the way that Jesus teaches, God is going to change you.

My friend, the greatest invitation imaginable has been extended to you. If you are a follower of Christ, the King of all kings who is the Sovereign Creator of the universe has adopted you into His family. Not only has He adopted you into His family, He has invited you to enter His presence any time you desire, and He has promised that as you enter His presence He will align your will with His. What's keeping you from accepting His invitation to experience greater intimacy with Him and to see your life radically transformed as you spend time with Him? Isn't it quite absurd that those of us who profess Christ spend so little time with Him? The death and resurrection of Jesus Christ has brought you into an intimate relationship with God the Father, and you can pray with boldness and assurance knowing He will change you.

> Let us then with confidence draw near to the throne of grace, that we may receive mercy and find grace to help in time of need. (Hebrews 4:16)

Jesus has given you a blueprint to show you how to encounter your Father in a life-changing way. Learn from the Master Teacher and do not neglect the wonderful gift of prayer you have been given.

7. As you finish reading this book, what excites you about disciplining yourself to learn to pray from Jesus? What overwhelms you?

8. In what ways have you seen God change your attitude through prayer?

9. How will knowing the goal of prayer — to be changed by God — change the way you pray?

Notes

INTRODUCTION

1. Collin Hansen and John Woodbridge, *A God-Sized Vision: Revival Stories that Stretch and Stir* (Grand Rapids: Zondervan Publishing House, 2010), 80-83; John Piper, *Desiring God* (Colorado Springs: Multnomah Publishers, Inc., 2003), 180-182.

CHAPTER 1

1. Ben Patterson and David L. Goetz, vol. 7, *Deepening Your Conversation with God* (Minneapolis, MN: Bethany House Publishers, 1999), 166-167.

2. Mark Galli and Ted Olsen, *131 Christians Everyone Should Know* (Nashville, TN: Broadman & Holman Publishers, 2000), 180.

CHAPTER 2

1. Kent Hughes, *The Sermon on the Mount* (Wheaton, IL: Crossway Books, 2001), 154.

2. Ibid.

3. J.I. Packer, *Knowing God* (Downers Grove, IL: IVP Books, 1973. Reprint 1993), 182.

CHAPTER 3

1. D. Martyn Lloyd Jones, *Studies in the Sermon on the Mount* (Grand Rapids: Wm. B. Eerdman's Publishing Company, 1976), 335.

CHAPTER 4

1. Hughes, *The Sermon on the Mount*, 170.

2. J. I. Packer, *Growing in Christ* (Wheaton, IL: Crossway Books, 1994), 176.

3 Ibid., 177.

CHAPTER 5

1. Eugene Meyers, "Adoniram Judson: Apostle of the Love of Christ in Burma" http://www.wholesomewords.org/missions/giants/biojudson2.html.

2. John Piper, *Adoniram Judson: How Few There Are Who Die So Hard!* (Minneapolis, MN: Desiring God, 2012), 7.

3. Ibid., 13-14.

4 Adoniram Judson, "Advice to Missionary Candidates," *Maulmain*, June 25, 1832, http://www.sholesomewords.org/missions/bjudson4.html.

CHAPTER 6

1. Timothy J. Keller, "Seeking the Kingdom" in *The Timothy Keller Sermon Archive* (New York City: Redeemer Presbyterian Church, 2013).

CHAPTER 7

1. Tullian Tchvidjian, "Forgiven People Forgive," *Liberate Blog*, August 6, 2013, accessed August 11, 2013, http://liberatenet.org/2013/08/06/forgiven-people-forgive/.

2. Ibid.

3. Ibid.

CHAPTER 9

1. Oswald Chambers, *My Utmost for His Highest: An Updated Edition in Today's Language* (Grand Rapids: Discovery House Publishers, 1992), August 28.

www.ingramcontent.com/pod-product-compliance
Lightning Source LLC
LaVergne TN
LVHW051831080426
835512LV00018B/2820